## PRAISE FOR MESSAGES FROM THE ARCHETYPES

"Toni Gilbert describes a very practical, hands on approach to Tarot. It is a good resource to anyone interested in the use of Tarot in self-development or as a tool for working with clients. Above all, I appreciate that the book is founded upon the philosophy that life can be experienced as a spiritual adventure. An adventure that holds great meaning."
  Robert Volkmann, MD, Transpersonal Counselor

"Toni makes it easy to see the similarity between Interactive Guided Imagery[SM] and Tarot. For those not familiar with the archetypes, her descriptive writing makes them easy to understand. I appreciate how she relates the metaphysical method of the Tarot with a psychological approach to healing. She lends credibility to Tarot's capacity to reveal emotional and psychological information from the level of the psyche. Her real life stories are alive and insightful."
Susan Ezra, RN, HNC, Beyond Ordinary Nursing

"*Messages from the Archetypes* explains Tarot, imagery, symbolism and synchronicity in such a clear way that any person unfamiliar with the cards would get it! I particularly like the way in which she weaves in different healing and energy modalities."
James Wanless, author, *Voyager Tarot* book and deck

"In *Messages from the Archetypes*, Ms. Gilbert defines the meeting-point between modern medicine and Tarot with enlightening results. Balancing her intuition and intellect against her solid grounding in holistic nursing she shows us how the traditional imagery of Tarot can spark interior associations leading to new realms of meaning and healing for both client and practitioner."
Christine Payne Towler, author, *The Underground Stream: Esoteric Tarot Revealed*

"Toni Gilbert deftly blends the complementary disciplines of nursing and the intuitive arts. Based upon synchronicity and a caring creative process, she allows the archetypal imagery of the Tarot to gently guide clients towards manifestation of their mental, physical and spiritual health."
Peter Moore, editor, *Alternatives for Cultural Creativity Magazine*

# MESSAGES
FROM THE
ARCHETYPES

From time to time you must consult old women,
gypsies, magicians, wayfarers
and all manner of peasant folk...
for these have more knowledge
[about wise conduct]
than all the high colleges.
PARACELSUS

# MESSAGES FROM THE ARCHETYPES

Using Tarot for Healing and Spiritual Growth
*A Guidebook for Personal and Professional Use*

by
TONI GILBERT, RN, MA, HNC

with
MARK ROBERT WALDMAN

WHITE CLOUD PRESS
ASHLAND, OREGON

Copyright © 2004 by Toni Gilbert
All rights reserved. No part of this book may be used or reproduced in any manner whatsoever without written permission except in the case of brief quotations embodied in critical articles and reviews.
Inquiries should be addressed to:
White Cloud Press, PO Box 3400, Ashland, Oregon 97520.
Website: www.whitecloudpress.com

First printing: 2004

Cover design by David Rupee
Printed in Malaysia

Cover Illustration by
Jonathan Webber

Library of Congress Cataloging-in-Publication Data

Gilbert, Toni.
Messages from the archetypes : using tarot for healing and spiritual growth : a guidebook for personal and professional use / by Toni Gilbert ; with Mark Robert Waldman.
p. cm.
Includes bibliographical references.
ISBN 1-883991-57-9
1. Tarot. 2. Archetype (Psychology) 3. Self-realization.
I. Waldman, Mark Robert. II. Title,
BF1879.T2G53 2003
133.3'2424--dc22
                                      2003022811

# Contents

Introduction: ... 5

SECTION I: THE HEALING ART OF TAROT
1. Exploring Tarot ... 9
2. Dream Work, Guided Imagery and Tarot ... 15
3. Tarot as an Inheritance ... 27
4. Conscious Archetypal Energy and Healing ... 44

SECTION II: USING TAROT IN HEALING
5. Getting Started ... 57
6. The Tarot Counselor ... 83
7. Tarot Case Stories ... 94

SECTION III: LEVELS OF THE ARCHETYPES
8. Archetypal Levels in Tarot Counseling ... 113
9. Levels of the Major Arcana ... 123
10. Levels of the Court Cards ... 139
11. Levels of the Minor Arcana ... 148

Epilogue ... 165
Appendix A ... 167
Appendix B ... 169

This work is dedicated to my grandmother
C. Esther Dickson-Gilbert-O'Neill
and
to my mentor in the art of Tarot counseling
Christine Payne Towler

# ACKNOWLEDGEMENTS

Mark Robert Waldman, my editor, writing mentor, trustworthy friend and old-fashioned agent. Working with him was an enriching experience for me and our readers will benefit. Lewis Judy, my best support person, intimate friend and partner for over thirty years. Christine Payne Towler, close friend, supporter and mentor in the art of Tarot counseling.

Robert Volkmann, MD, an alternative doctor and confidante who shares my love of life's innermost mysteries. Sarah Duval, PMHNP, not just another nurse, but a long-time friend, script reader and advisor. Patrick Hart, DC, doctor, editor and manuscript consultant who shared his creative ideas. Peter Moore, editor, intimate friend and catalyst for my personal and professional growth. He encouraged me to write and published my first article in his magazine *Alternatives for Cultural Creativity*.

Winifred Morris, writer of many children's books, friend and professional advisor. Trudy Webb, a client manuscript reader, an ally and tireless champion of integrative therapies. Johnny Lake, aka Asanté, a long-time best friend and my window into the African American worldview.

Eric Dalkenberg, a friend, manuscript reader and a computer whiz when I need one. Jonathan Webber, the talented cover artist and excellent symbologist.

Claire, my electronic companion…my computer.

I Am Healer<br>
I Am Healed<br>
I Am Above

# Introduction

Years ago, during a mid-life crisis, I found myself attracted to a man who was not my husband. I was the emotional captive of a pair of beautiful eyes and an inviting smile. After exhausting my storehouse of coping skills, I searched my home for a Tarot deck I had purchased in San Francisco many years before. I had always been curious about Tarot cards but somehow they didn't feel right. Whenever I would approach the cards and try to intellectually "figure them out," I would feel energetically drained, but with this mid-life crisis my heart, as well as my brain, needed answers.

Suddenly, my perception was opened in a way I had never experienced, for the cards' symbolism spoke to me through my intuition, mirroring what I was feeling with astonishing accuracy. They gave me the insights to manage my emotions and move through the attraction without causing damage to my marriage.

I began experimenting on friends and family, and to my astonishment, they invariably found that Tarot readings clarified their issues. Some, however, did not appreciate my latest esoteric interest. My son Ryan, for example, would not let me read his cards. "I'm a grown man," he said, "and I don't want my mother getting into my head." Teasingly, he threatened to put a sign in my front yard: a giant hand with the words "Tarot Reader" printed across the palm.

My longtime friend, Sarah, was so against Tarot that she refused to look at the images on the cards—she followed a conservative religion that forbade them. However, most of the people I met and worked with were open to this type of counseling.

I loved experimenting with the cards but the scientific part of my brain wanted to know more. Thus began a journey with remarkable teachers and authors who were not afraid to express their truths. As I studied Tarot, my intuition and intellect were operating at peak performance. Like a sponge I collected data from my observations and experiences. I was also supported by friends who allowed me to observe their psyche while observing the cards, and I was graced with mentors who knew more than I and were willing to show me the way.

This book is based upon an archetypal system of healing that has been used for centuries as a form of divination and over the years I have found it to be an effective form of therapy. In my holistic nursing practice, I often see clients in crisis due to illness, injury or difficult life issues and I discovered that I could use the Tarot cards to accurately reflect my client's present state of mind. In combination with the transpersonal counseling process, the cards have become one of my most efficient tools.

In this book, we will explore how to use Tarot as a therapeutic tool using well-known principles garnered from transpersonal psychology. In particular, the works of Carl Jung and Abraham Maslow have contributed to the hypotheses that Tarot can be used to facilitate a profound transformative process, one that unfolds for both practitioner and client.

In Section One, I will demonstrate how Tarot reflects an accurate psychological profile for whomever the cards are dealt. Section Two will outline my method of counseling with the cards and offer several case studies. Lastly, Section Three explains the symbology and the levels of archetypal expression for each card in the Tarot deck.

Tarot is a complex system and those who aspire to work with such imagery will approach it differently, depending upon who they are and the varying gifts and talents they bring to the process. Some practitioners approach it intellectually or cognitively; others approach it intuitively or psychically and some approach it both ways.

I hope that my passion for the study of Tarot will inspire you to experiment with this consciousness-raising tool, a tool that anyone can use to become aware of his or her innate intuition. Tarot teaches us how to bring greater understanding into our lives and can be a useful in our search for wholeness and health.

For nearly a decade, Tarot has been both companion and friend, a spiritual art that I have successfully used with my family, friends and clients to facilitate inner-world explorations. I feel a sublime gratitude for this sacred privilege and I approach it with great respect. The implications for its use in psychotherapy can be far-reaching and I hope that this book will guide you into that wonderful realm of archetypal consciousness and perennial wisdom.

REPRINTED TAROT IMAGES
*Tarot Images* reprinted with permission from:
Osho International, images/text taken from the Osho Zen Tarot: The Transcendental Game of Zen, by Osho. 1995 St. Martin's Press, New York ISBN 0312117337
Online reading available at www.osho.com

*Voyager Tarot: Way of the Great Oracle*, by James Wanless and artist Ken Knutson. Merrill-West Publishing, Carmel, CA ISBN 0-9615079-3-4
Available online at www.voyagertarot.com

Illustrations from the Rider-Waite Tarot Deck, known also as the Rider Tarot and the Waite Tarot, reproduced by permission of U.S. Games Systems, Inc., Stamford, CT 06902 USA. Copyright 1971 by U.S. Games Systems, Inc. Further reproduction prohibited. The Rider-Waite Tarot Deck is a registered trademark of U.S. Games Systems, Inc. www.usgamesinc.com

## That I Am

Often, I go off wandering…wondering
    Often, I find a treasure there
    Often, I see…
    Often, I feel…
    Often, I hear…
    Often, I sense…
I Am the I Am
    I Am Imagination
    I Am Time
I Am Love
    I Am Student
    I Am Teacher
    I Am Healer
    I Am Healed
    I Am Above
    I Am Below
    I Am Ego
    I Am She
    I Am He
    I Am Big
    I Am Small
    I Am All that Is
    I Am The All

*Toni Gilbert - 2000*

Section One

# The Healing Art of Tarot

*Often, I go off wandering…wondering*
*Often, I find a treasure there*
*Often, I see…*
*Often, I feel…*
*Often, I hear…*
*Often, I sense…*
*I Am the I Am*

Chapter One

# Exploring Tarot

**T**EARS BURST FORTH and flowed down her cheeks when she saw the image of the sorrowful man on the face of the Tarot card. "I have felt like that for so long," she said. Jan had shuffled the deck of seventy-eight cards and the sorrowful image was the first of a four-card spread. She had come seeking answers beyond the realm of traditional medicine because it held no further treatment options for her condition. She had recently been diagnosed with an irreversible degenerative condition of the eye and felt her only hope was to arrest the progression and prevent blindness.

There I was, a health care professional, sitting barefoot on the floor! I had placed Tarot cards, gypsy style, between the client and myself. We sat on small pillows, with bright purple and yellow sarongs spread out beneath us. I know it sounds funny but somehow, it felt right and very feminine to be counseling in this way. It made me feel more like a barefoot healer getting down to the "real" part of the issues rather than a nurse quietly listening from a chair.

Not only was I acting outside my normal professional role, but I was also a first time participant at one of Breitenbush's annual retreats. Breitenbush is an alternative community situated high in the Oregon mountains. It has a conference and retreat center that plays host to teachers like Ram Dass, Andrew Weil and Hank Wesselman. These events not only provide revenue to keep the community alive, but offer people simple hope in a complex world.

For me, this venture into alternative medicine was to be personally and professionally rewarding. I came to the healing solstice, to be with and observe alternative practitioners but, in particular, I wanted to explore the use of Tarot with physically ill clients who were in a spiritual or emotional crisis. At the time, Tarot was not a nursing modality, and I didn't feel right about experimenting with paying clients.

I had been exploring the use of Tarot with my family and friends for years. I knew the cards were catalytic, for time after time, I saw their faces light up in "ah ha" responses to the images on the cards. It definitely moved their thinking towards insights about the issue in question.

So far, the results of this very old counseling process seemed quite magical. I knew it was time to push the edge in my explorations and I needed a test group. In coming to Breitenbush I thought I would find a few willing participants who would allow me to explore the use of the cards as a therapeutic tool in wellness counseling. How could they best be used? I offered Tarot sessions free of charge, and in exchange I got to practice on clients who had come in search of alternative healing.

On my first day, the June sun was shining outside a building called the Vista House, where I was receiving clients. The resin on the surrounding trees gave off a wonderful therapeutic aroma as it warmed in the sun. I could literally feel what seemed like an all-encompassing angelic presence in the air and the environment caused me to instinctively breathe in deep to receive the higher energy of this peaceful place. I felt satisfied to the core just being there.

The Vista House is a small wooden cottage located to one side of the central old lodge and close to the river, and I was seeing clients in the upper Sky Room. The only access was a weathered set of steps on the outside of the building. Inside, on one of the lavender painted walls, was a large gold and purple tapestry with row-upon-row of powerful elephants saluting each other. In the corner was a massage table, with two low dressers that held linens and other supplies.

Jan had signed up for a Tarot reading. She knew that I was certified in a guided imagery technique, and she was open to the use of the cards, but she also wanted to explore the possibilities of Interactive Guided Imagery$^{sm}$ (IGI) in regard to her eye condition.

Jan was clearly in an emotional crisis. She told me about her medical diagnosis of a degenerative condition of the eye. When the cards were laid out on the floor, she identified with the sorrowful man because it reflected her sadness and hopelessness about her condition. The next card portrayed a scenic painting of a pleasant looking woman walking in nature, holding a basket of flowers. The title of the card was "ordinariness," which reminded her of her career, for she described herself as a rather bland art teacher. The third card contained a picture of someone in a narrow and dark confined space, all tied up in heavy ropes; a block of smoky clouds obscured the head. The descriptive title was "suppression." This card, combined with the information of the second card, were strong images, prompting her to discuss how she, a longtime art teacher, did not feel connected with her high school students. She did an adequate job, but she felt deeply unfulfilled as an artist and teacher. The fourth and last card, which usually has to do with a client's hopes or fears, was titled "beyond illusion." This abstractly beautiful card showed a serene face in meditation imposed over a yellow butterfly on a background of deep blue sky. It also had a multitude of sparkling light images radiating from the butterfly. To her, the image seemed filled with positive energy. On the forehead of the face and between the wings of the butterfly there rested a feminine oval shape that gradually rippled down to a small, soft circle between the eyebrows. She saw this as an image of creativity being born from her mind much like a butterfly from a caterpillar. I pointed out that the area she identified was in the sixth Chakra.

The Chakra system is a traditional energy model that has been used throughout Asia for centuries. The sixth Chakra is one of the seven core energy centers that form the coordinating network of our complicated mind-body system. All our actions and understandings are thought to arise from these multiple points of energy within ourselves. Full of information, they form connecting links between mind and body, spirit and matter, past and future.

The Chakra system provides an excellent framework for assessing not only the mind and body but also the spiritual aspects of the client as well. Jan and I discussed the symbolic implications of the sixth Chakra located between the brows, which is associated with intuition and the physiological functioning of the eyes.

As a holistic practitioner, I guide clients into the emotional and spiritual aspects of their illness using the Tarot to help open an intimate discussion. My dialogue with Jan sparked a profound emotional disclosure about her feelings. She not only talked about her medical condition, but her life's work as well. Her body, from her shoulders to her waist, rounded into a C-shape as she cried softly and told me of her despair over her doctor's prognosis. I stayed calm and talked to her in a soothing and supportive way, holding a space for her to express intense feelings. We explored her emotions as we talked through the issues the Tarot reading brought up. The last card, with the butterfly image, and the resulting discussion about intuition, gave her hope. I sensed a certain peacefulness come over her.

After several minutes of careful listening, my observations and intuition told me she was once again in control. She was sitting straight and strong and I could tell by her calm expression and good eye contact that she was feeling emotional relief. Her solid ego strength was evident in her willingness and courage to explore other dimensions of her self in an attempt to find healing.

At the time, my experience with Interactive Guided Imagery or IGI spanned over a decade. As a therapeutic tool, it taps into the deeper layers of the psyche bringing forth unconscious information. It does this by directing the client through a progressive relaxation to a meditative place in which he or she can be receptive to deeper insights and images. In such a state, the counselor can ask appropriate questions to facilitate the client's imaginings. In the imagination, IGI can make use of all of the senses: seeing, hearing, smelling, feeling, touching, and intuition.

In my work, I was beginning to see similarities between the effects of IGI and the effects of Tarot, for they both produced results by bridging unconscious information from the storehouse of the client's own experience to the conscious ego. I explained to Jan how IGI could inspire insights that could empower her and I assured her that she would be in complete control. If at anytime she felt uncomfortable she needed only to open her eyes. Feeling assured, she lay out on the floor and closed her eyes.

I used a meditation technique to help her reach a relaxed state. I slowly led her to focus her attention upon her muscles, relaxing them one at a time, from the top of her head down to her feet. I could see her body go lax as she followed my suggestions. When she was ready, I told her to go to a special place in her imagination where she could dialogue with an inner healer. She found herself in a peaceful forest where she explored her surroundings and eventually found her inner healer.

Inner healers come in many forms. They can be people, places, animals or inanimate objects. As it turned out, Jan's inner healer was a pond of cool clear water. With her eyes still closed, she identified the pond as a symbolic representation of her emotions and of spiritual healing. I asked her to communicate with the pond. Since ponds don't talk, she communed telepathically. The pond told her to become more aware of her intuition, to live and feel her art instead of painting and drawing only from the intellect. Through this inner healer Jan gained both insight and a plan to help her become more intuitive, creative, and spontaneous with her students.

After the guided imagery session, we discussed her insights and mapped out a detailed plan. Instead of trying to tightly control her students' drawings, she decided to encourage them to play with symbols and abstract forms. She also explored ways to introduce more spontaneity in her own artwork. She felt a fondness for the pond, and she wanted to reproduce it by placing a bowl of water on her home alter. As a daily ritual, she planned to dab water from the bowl onto her eyes and the sixth Chakra as a reminder of her desire to bring true artistic living into her life. For Jan, it was both a surprise and a great relief to come up with an easy plan of action.

After the imagery session, I talked to Jan about how the eye condition might be linked to her neglect of her intuitive nature. I felt that the life force of her sixth Chakra may have slowed or become blocked contributing to weakened tissues and the resulting eye degeneration. She agreed and was intent on changing her ways of being in the world. The session ended and we stood up to say our good-byes in front of the saluting elephant tapestry, a last grateful embrace coming straight from our hearts.

The teaching worked both ways. She gained an awareness of her intuitive self and hope for healing and I took one more step towards the use of Tarot in wellness counseling.

As a certified holistic nurse with a master's degree in transpersonal studies, I approach wellness counseling using healing arts techniques to help clients gain insights about their physical ailments. As in the session described above, I bring Tarot in as a tool for my initial assessment. With the cards, I gather information from a client's reactions to the images, seeing them as a reflection of the client's mental and emotional states, including their hopes and fears. These may come true in the course of the client's life, but I see them as only possibilities at the time of the reading. Time and time again I have observed a mysterious synchronicity as the cards fall in place accurately depicting the client's issue as they question and search for an answer. Although Tarot cannot be fully explained in a scientific and materialistic manner, I approach this time-honored system with a deep respect and have learned to trust the mystery of the cards.

Chapter Two

# Dream Work, Guided Imagery, and Tarot

*I Am Imagination*

**D**REAMS HAVE NOT only helped individuals in personal crisis but have influenced leaders in politics and battle throughout history. The Bible's Old and New Testaments contain many references and countless stories about dreams. The Hebrew people considered them to be direct and powerful experiences of God, and Daniel was said to have had an understanding of all forms of visions and dreams.

One of my favorite stories describes how Daniel took charge of a volatile situation which endangered his life. Daniel was considered gifted and was the king's counselor. Everything was peaceful and safe, when suddenly a catastrophe arose. The king had a nightmare.

King Nebuchadnezar awoke, trembling with fear. He declared, "I've had a terrible nightmare," he said to his magicians, incantationists, sorcerers, and astrologers, as they stood before him, "and I can't remember what it was. Tell me, for I fear some tragedy awaits me."

The astrologers said to the king, "Sir, tell us the dream and then we can tell you what it means."

The king replied, "I tell you, the dream is gone—I can't remember it. And if *you* won't tell me what it was and what it means,

I'll have you torn limb from limb and your houses made into heaps of rubble." He commanded the magicians, astrologers, sorcerers and the Chaldeans to step forward. " I will give you many wonderful gifts and honors if you tell me what the dream was and what it means. So begin!"

Being of the honest sort, they said, "How can we tell you what the dream means unless you tell us what it was?" They needed more information. They needed to know what important symbols the king's dream contained.

This infuriated Nebuchadnezar. "I can see your trick! You're trying to stall for time until the calamity befalls me that the dream foretells. But if you don't tell me the dream, you certainly can't expect me to believe your interpretation!"

What kind of servants were they if they couldn't interpret the king's dream! The Chaldeans said to the king, "There is not a man upon the earth who can show the king's matter. There is no king, lord, nor ruler, who has ever asked such things from any magician, or astrologer, or Chaldean. It is a rare thing that the king requireth, and none other except the gods, whose dwelling is not with the flesh can show it to you."

The King then threatened to execute all the wise men of Babylon.

Daniel went before the king and said, "Give me a little time and I will tell you the dream and what it means." That night, Daniel received the secret of the dream in a vision given to him by God.

He went before Nebuchadnezar and said, "O king, you saw a huge and powerful statue of a man, shining brilliantly, frightening and terrible. The head of the statue was made of purest gold, its chest and arms were of silver, its belly and thighs of brass, legs of iron, its feet part iron and part clay. But as you watched, a rock was cut from the mountainside by supernatural means. It came hurtling toward the statue and crushed the feet of iron and clay, smashing them to bits. Then the whole statue collapsed into a heap of iron, clay, brass, silver, and gold; its pieces were crushed as small as chaff, and the wind blew them all away. But the rock that knocked the statue down became a great mountain that covered the whole earth."

Daniel then proceeded to interpret the vision. "Your Majesty, you are a king over many kings, for the God of heaven has given you your kingdom, power, strength and glory. You rule the farthest provinces, and even animals and birds are under your control, as God decreed. You are that head of gold." Gold, in Daniel's interpretation, is represented as "...power, strength and glory" as it is to us today. When an image has the same meaning in all cultures and across time it is known as an archetypal symbol.

Tarot is also a system that has archetypal symbols, which everyone can resonate with. We resonate with them because they contain essential elements of our being—our hopes, fears, strengths, and weaknesses of our bodies, minds, and spirit. These same images can come to us through dreams and when we use guided imagery. All three modalities draw upon the archetypal energies that are hidden within deeper levels of our consciousness.

Daniel's interpretation continued, "Its chest and arms were of silver, its belly and thighs of brass, its legs of iron, its feet part iron and part clay." Of this Daniel intuited, "But after your kingdom has come to an end, another world power will arise to take your place. This empire will be inferior to yours. And after that kingdom has fallen, yet a third great power —represented by the bronze belly of the statue— will rise to rule the world.

"Following it, the fourth kingdom will be strong as iron—smashing, bruising and conquering." This part of Daniel's interpretation used the physical characteristics of the metal metaphorically. Metaphors, like images, hold symbolic meaning and help people find words to describe their inner feelings and thoughts. The metaphoric phrase above is archetypal because it has the same meaning to all people across time.

As in dreams, guided imagery and Tarot many symbols appear that hold archetypal value for the person who seeks healing advice. For instance, the Star of David, which appears on certain cards, holds significance to many people. Physically, one triangle of the star strives upward, toward the heavens, while another strives downward, toward man. This can mean many things: a symbol for the meeting of heaven and earth, "thy will be done," or our capacity to reach for and grasp stars—our destiny, our dreams, our hopes.

Daniel's interpretation continued, "The feet and toes you saw —part iron and part clay show that later on, this kingdom will be divided. Some parts of it will be as strong as iron, and some as weak as clay. This mixture of iron with clay also shows that these kingdoms will try to strengthen themselves by forming alliances with each other through intermarriage of their ruler. But this will not succeed, for iron and clay don't mix." Daniel seems to be prophesizing about the political failure of future generations.

In contemporary psychology, this would be called a precognitive dream, in which the events of the dream come before the events that actually take place in the reality of the world. In his interpretation Daniel seems to be prophesizing the future, about which we can only speculate.

Daniel finished by saying, "Thus the great God has shown what will happen in the future, and this interpretation of your dream is as sure and certain as my description of it."

Although it can look like he played up to the narcissism of the king to save their skins, I find the symbolism of the dream and the interpretation brilliant for it shows us that a creative interpretation can give us a new way of seeing ourselves and the world. It may even save someone's life. If we trust our intuition, we begin to see that our dreams and our interpretations can become useful tools for tapping into the archetypal realms.

Dreams hold special meanings for the dreamer. In the past, many benefited from the spiritual or the intuitive arts, especially dreaming kings. It reminds us that there are other ways, both past and present, to guide us towards wellness and health.

Robert, a physician, was an avid dream worker. Every morning he would diligently write down his dreams. If Nebuchadnezar had been as diligent as Robert about writing down his dreams we wouldn't have received his wonderful archetypal story to teach us. We would just have Daniel and his lion. I was soon to find out that Robert had a lion, too.

When Robert discovered that I worked with the symbolic images of the nighttime, he asked me to join him. Being busy professionals, we didn't have time to get together as people usually do when working with dreams, so he suggested that we exchange dream imagery by e-mail. I agreed but wasn't sure it would work. Usually, my intuitive insights were achieved, in part, by watching the dreamer's subtle body language and facial expressions, but Robert was asking me to do something entirely different. I didn't know how to proceed.

Before I tell you about Robert's dream, I would like to give the imagination the measure of respect it deserves. The imaginal realm is an incredible tool, through which the Christian mystic, Hildegard of Bingen, said God spoke to her using voice and images. Like Hildegard, I believe that we too can receive spiritual information in our imaginings.

Every man-made object that you see was first conceived of in someone's imagination. This is also true of conceptual theories, philosophy, religion, psychology and so on. The highly imaginative are often called visionary. If you look closely at your imagination, you *must* pause and ask, "Whose imagination conceived of us?"

Robert sent me a detailed dream scenario. I e-mailed back, "I don't think I can work with dreams in this way. I am used to more of an interactive situation with the dreamer in which I get immediate feedback." In reply he suggested, "Just try sitting in meditation and see what comes up in the imagery of your imagination."

I remembered the story of Daniel and imagined the way in which he might have worked. It made sense that he would go off by himself, finding a quiet place where he would be undisturbed as he prayed and meditated. In this receptive state, he would then be open for interpretations to dream symbols. The Bible tells us that in King Nebuchadnezar's case, Daniel received divine guidance.

Exactly how God chose to reveal this information to Daniel is not clear. It does seem that he prayed and waited, which put him into a more receptive state. Did he use active imagination and guided imagery? Did inner healers appear in his imagination to give advice? The information came to Daniel as a vision in the night, and this piqued my curiosity.

In all my years of dreamwork, it had never occurred to me to meditate *in the night* upon another's dreams. The technique was familiar; Carl Jung called it *active imagination*. Active imagination was a precursor to today's guided imagery techniques.

I began my experiment, but told Robert to take my impressions with a grain of salt. I didn't want to cause harm with my lively imagination. He had agreed and said he would take only what was useful to him and disregard the rest. Thus began an intimate journey into the world of dreams.

In Robert's first dream, he found himself in a homeless shelter. He had been traveling and couldn't find a place to sleep. He ended up at the Union Gospel Mission. He wrote that he was "feeling drunk, or at least, I was so weak on my legs, that I crawled back into the far corner looking for a place to sleep, but realized that I didn't belong there as it was where the homeless had their religious services." His dream monologue went on to talk about not wanting to sleep with the other derelicts because he might get scabies and lice.

It was my turn. I said a short prayer for guidance and sat in meditation, holding Robert's dream in my mind. After a minute or two I settled into a deeper level of consciousness. "Is there anyone who will come forward to give information to Robert regarding this dream?" I asked. I waited expectantly for an answer. Almost instantly, an image of a lion sitting on his haunches appeared. I asked the lion if he had come to help. He looked at me, got up and walked away, farting as he went. I thought to myself, "This is strange." I then received a telepathic message from the

## Using Tarot for Healing and Spiritual Growth

departing lion that Robert's dream insinuated a lack of courage and low self-esteem. The lion's farting was a symbol of his disapproval.

I then asked if anyone else would come forward to help with Robert's dream. Lo and behold, Merlin the magician appeared. He had white hair and a beard, and was dressed in a beautiful purple cape with rich ermine trim. He looked magnificent, standing in a slow swirling energy that moved through his hair, beard and cape. He stood as the magician on the Tarot card with one hand pointed towards the heavens and stars, and with the other, downward in the direction of the earthly plane.

Merlin said that Robert was a valued son. "Tell him that he is in the process of learning the ways of the world as well as the ways of the spiritual plane. He should not give up, for his efforts at this time should be towards the practice of positive thinking."

Merlin continued, "Negative thinking is of the lower plane. You should bring your spirituality into the world like the magician. Think of your efforts at positive thinking as your higher self." He then cautioned against the arrogance Robert might fall into while involved in spiritual work.

Merlin then said to Robert, "Get a material symbol to remind you of the higher level of thinking, putting it in places that will remind you of what you need." He then held out his hand. On the upturned palm sat a multifaceted crystal that shone brightly with rainbows of lights emanating from it. In a final gesture he magically faded from my view. I knew he was finished.

I sent the message to Robert by e-mail. There was silence. Was I accurate? Did he think I was crazy? Did I hit a nerve? The only thing indicating that I was on the right track were the images symbolizing issues of the lower Chakras: weak legs, lack of belonging and not finding a place to sleep. I saw these as indicative of safety and security issues, as well as belonging and self-esteem. Because the shelter was called Union Gospel Mission, a place where religious services were held, spiritual issues of the upper Chakras (higher planes of awareness) were making themselves evident. I knew from our three-year friendship that Robert had insecurities and a sensitivity, which he protected with a certain guardedness. My meditation seemed to address them. He didn't give me direct feedback, and I gave him space to reflect. Surprisingly, the next day my e-mail box looked like this:

| Robert | my dream |
| Robert | my day dream |
| Robert | my noon dream |
| Robert | my dream lover |
| Robert | a dream in 1986 |
| Robert | another dream |
| Robert | a dream in 1999 |
| Robert | one more dream |
| Robert | how about this one? |
| Robert | two dreams |

Robert wrote down several dreams a night and had several for years recorded them in his journals. I began receiving about four e-mailed dreams a day from Robert. By this gesture I understood that the information was well received.

When Robert interpreted my dreams in a similar fashion, I also received new perspectives and insights. His interpretations were thought-provoking, making us both more confident about working with dreams in a meditative state.

Most contemporary dreamwork is accomplished by direct counseling, helping clients come to their own interpretations through personal associations. The aim when working with our own and other's dreams is to interpret the dream images in a way that gives important information and insights to the dreamer. Once again, I had stepped over a traditional threshold and into a new way of working with dreams.

Dreamwork is an ancient healing art that is used in medicine today, for dreams often contain symbolic messages that come in service of healing. The subtle sensations that the dreamer experiences can tell both the health care provider and the dreamer what's happening in the body during a period of injury or disease. For instance, I dreamt of my car parked with doors open. The headlights and dome light were dim, indicating a run down battery. As was true in my waking life, my physical body was tired and low on energy.

The dreamer can also learn to contact unrecognized emotions. Information in the dream can empower clients to understand reactions to treatment so they can express their emotions and rid themselves of its negative impact. When emotions are brought to waking consciousness the dreamer is able to express them more effectively. This can be cathartic and help in relieving symptoms.

Dreams can teach clients how to contact the curative powers within the mind. With a technique called incubation, the dreamer can pray or ask the dreaming mind before going to sleep for personal healing symbols. The healing symbols received from the dream will have special significance in the dreamer's life. They may even bring curative solutions. The client should be encouraged to work with the healing dream symbols, by drawing them using art materials or other methods of contemplation. For example, Lisa dreamt of a dolphin, named Bill, and to Lisa he felt like a nurturing helper that came to give her comfort as she battled cancer. She purchased a small pewter dolphin that fit into the palm of her hand and carried it around in her pocket. She could easily reach in and feel its smooth surface. By touching the dolphin she was reminded of the feeling in the dream and of having Bill near, which gave her comfort. Thus healing symbols can bring the positive feelings of the dream to the waking consciousness, which as we know, affects the immune system, and in turn, speeds healing.

If a dream symbol is particularly significant one might encourage the client to work with the image/symbol for weeks or months for maximum benefit. As clients move forward in their healing, their images change. Lisa worked with the image of the dolphin for several months and eventually integrated Bill's feeling of nurturing as being a part of her personality. He then no longer appeared in her dreams or imagery.

The dream also can help the health professional assess progress in stages of healing. Clients often report images of green plant growth in their dreams as they recover from illness or injury. Positive "new growth" in various forms usually indicatives an inner and outer healing. For instance, a client might relate a dream in which they are watering their favorite plants. To them, the plants looked bigger and healthier than they ever had. If healthy plants represent health, what important information does this give you in regard to the body's condition? Water is an archetypal emotional symbol. What might it connote? Self healing? Courage? Faith? The feeling sense of the dream can also give you additional clues. If the feeling was of well-being and pride it would tell you that healing was in process.

My grandmother, a Christian minister well-versed in the healing arts, introduced me to the concept of dreamwork when I was a pre-adolescent. At nearly six feet tall, she had a commanding presence, and because of her interest in me, was a big influence on my budding awareness. Her life's work and the stories she told gave my imagination a boost in working with the magically symbolic images of the mind.

As I remember, she used energy work on clients who came to her home. Through her hands, she told me, ran healing energy. This art, she said was, the "laying on of hands."

Once, I saw a man in a wheelchair in her home. She told me he came often for treatment. He had a special relationship with my grandmother and she told me about a spiritual connection they shared. This was holistic care being practiced in the fifties! Twenty years after her death, I clearly see my grandmother reflected in myself, and my own work.

My grandmother also had knowledge of the "occult arts," which in the fifties, was a very new idea. To some Christians, interpretation of dreams was considered the work of the devil, a notion that dates back to the fifth century, when radicals within the church lead people to believe that interpreting dreams was akin to witchcraft. But my open-minded grandmother did not believe it was sinful and I listened in rapt attention as she explained how they hold special meanings to people who approach dreams with respect. I can still see her eyes through her rose-tinted glasses as she spoke of the seriousness of dreams.

My grandmother talked about the dreaming level of consciousness as a universe of energies, forces, and distinct personalities that live within us. It is a larger realm than we realize, one that has a complete life of its own. This place in us is the source of much of our thought, feeling and behavior, and it has a powerful influence because it is unconscious. Most people, my grandmother said, do not give this level of consciousness the attention and respect it deserves.

As a child, I had a vivid imagination, and so my dreams were plentiful and I started paying attention to those characters that came to me in the night. I developed a relationship with my dreaming friends, and I looked forward to them as I fell asleep. Grandmother told me that everything in a dream held special meaning for the dreamer, but my immature mind could not make sense out of them at the time. Still, they continued to hold my attention until, in my early twenties, my symbolic thinking, and ability to interpret my dreams, began to develop.

Symbols are pregnant with meaning and may include objects with shapes, such as a cross or a circle, animals like a bear or a fish, places like a home or a meadow in nature, vehicles like a bicycle or a bus, or people like Indian warriors and angels.

Symbolic thinking is the ability to look at a symbol and instantly *know* that it has meaning. When I see a symbol, I feel a certain subtle energetic sensation, which I identify as intuition. For me, it is at the gut level, or the solar plexus of my body. Almost instantly my intellect brings the felt meaning of that symbol to my waking consciousness.

Symbolic meanings can be personal, collective, or universal. A personal meaning is one that holds ideas and feelings in your life experience. A collective meaning is one in which the meaning is the same to a larger group of people. Universal meanings hold the same information across all cultures and throughout time.

As an advanced practitioner of dreamwork, guided imagery, and Tarot I can see the similarities between all three therapies. There are important meanings behind the images, and the images themselves come from the same unconscious and preconscious states of the mind. Unlike dreams and guided imagery, the Tarot image is on the outside of the person and on a card. The symbolic image is first visible to the conscious level of the mind.

These three therapeutic tools—dreamwork, guided imagery, and Tarot—tap into non-rational aspects of our consciousness bringing hidden information to our awareness. Unlike dreams and guided imagery, Tarot has had little research, and unfortunately conjures up images of gypsies. Sadly, this useful tool continues to remain shrouded in an occult, fortune-telling mystique.

Chapter Three

# Tarot as an Inheritance

*I Am Time*

THE TRADITION OF Tarot deserves to be approached with respect for it is more than a deck of cards with symbolic images applied to the faces. As one of the oldest known methods of counseling, these cards have survived the changing elements of time. Over the years, they have taken on many alterations, while continuing to communicate their archetypal wisdom.

Throughout history, people have developed various systems of storytelling to pass on their knowledge. Important cultural events, with their local heroes and villains, made their way into the tales. The village storytellers expressed what they heard from others and passed on what they witnessed in the forms of myths, legends and fables. These archetypal modes of communication were transmitted from grandparent to grandchild, generation after generation until they were recorded in books, drama, and works of art.

Tarot was one of the ways that people passed along their wisdom and philosophical beliefs.

Tarot, as we know it today, emerged from a collection of seventy-eight cards developed in the fifteenth century. The first twenty-two pictorial cards are called the Major Arcana and are numbered from one through twenty-one, with a beginning card that is either unnumbered or labeled zero. The images on each card carry a rich symbolic tapestry of human experience.

## The Rider-Waite Major Arcana

USING TAROT FOR HEALING AND SPIRITUAL GROWTH

The next sixteen court cards are called the Minor Arcana and resemble a standard playing deck. In a modern deck the four suits are labeled clubs, hearts, spades and diamonds. In Tarot, the archetypal kings, queens, knights and pages are also depicted in four suits but here they are called Wands, Cups, Swords and Pentacles.

In some decks the names of the suits are different. For example, Wands may be called fire, Cups can become water, Swords are renamed air, and Pentacles may be changed to earth or coins. Whatever the name, the basic energy of the suit remains the same and is reflected in the archetype of each card.

Generally speaking, Cups represent our emotional state, Wands symbolize energy and creativity, Swords refer to our thoughts and plans, and Pentacles stand for the way we manifest ourselves in the physical world.

The Court cards represent different parts of our personality. The Queen of Wands, for example, can symbolize a woman who has feminine charm and grace, one who is intuitive, creative and capable of sustaining a vision until completion. At the lower levels of this archetype, the card can represent a woman who is unorganized, temperamental and stubbornly willful. The King of Hearts can represent a man who is in touch with his feelings and seeks to form relationships. At the lower levels it can represent a man who seeks relationships that feed his ego. The Knight of Swords can stand for a person who has a new idea. At the lower levels it can signify one who has poorly thought out ideas. The Page of Pentacles can symbolize a youth with a beginning awareness of the senses and his body. At the lower levels this card can indicate an immaturity and fear of disapproval.

## The Rider-Waite Court Cards

| KING of CUPS. | QUEEN of CUPS. | KNIGHT of CUPS. | PAGE of CUPS. |

USING TAROT FOR HEALING AND SPIRITUAL GROWTH

| KING of PENTACLES. |  QUEEN of PENTACLES. |  KNIGHT of PENTACLES. |  PAGE of PENTACLES. |
|  KING of SWORDS. |  QUEEN of SWORDS. |  KNIGHT of SWORDS. |  PAGE of SWORDS. |
|  KING of WANDS. |  QUEEN of WANDS. |  KNIGHT of WANDS. |  PAGE of WANDS. |

The remaining forty Minor Arcana cards, in the suits of Wands, Cups, Swords and Pentacles are numbered ace through ten and symbolize archetypal situations in which we find ourselves. They are basic scenarios we play out as we go about our

## Messages from the Archetypes

daily lives. For example, the Ace of Cups may symbolize the purest aspect of emotional energy and the moving power behind the spiritual. The Five of Wands can represent obstacles that occur in the course of creative work. The Nine of Cups can be indicative of internal and external well-being. The Ten of Swords often indicates a decision to end something.

### The Rider-Waite Numbered Minor Arcana

## Using Tarot for Healing and Spiritual Growth

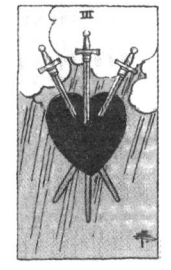

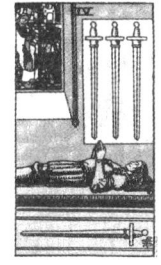

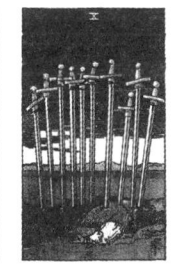

## The Rider-Waite Numbered Minor Arcana (continued)

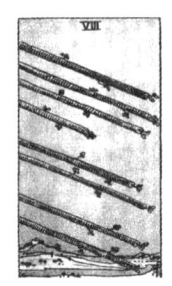

The images of Tarot represent archetypal principles that are collectively experienced regardless of cultural conditioning or family imprinting. Each of us is a unique combination of these archetypal principles. Our roles and the clothes we wear reflect and affect the archetypal energy at work in us. For instance, the uniform of a policeman contributes to his archetypal feelings and behavior. (He wouldn't feel like a policeman in jeans and sandals.) In Tarot, the King of Swords represents someone who likes his world in order and could, therefore, symbolize the officer's personality traits. When the officer goes home and puts on relaxed clothing his feelings and behaviors change. Taking on the role of good parent he extends love to his children and allows them to love him in return. In this instance, he expresses yet another archetypal principle, the higher levels of the King of Cups. If he gives too much to the child and doesn't take time for himself, he expresses the lower levels of this archetype.

The archetypes of the Major Arcana in the classic Rider-Waite deck, can be seen as a story about the hero's journey towards self-actualization. Each card symbolizes a progression through developing stages of awareness, psychological growth, maturity, and integration. In the hero's journey we find the courage to overcome obstacles in the mind and heart, as well as challenges we encounter in the world.

Using Tarot for Healing and Spiritual Growth

THE JOURNEY BEGINS with The Fool, the first archetypal card in the Tarot deck. She is no ordinary fool but one that harkens to an inner call to growth and maturity.

She is naïve but she has the courage to begin a journey into the unknown territory of her being, her unconscious self. She begins to notice her dreams. She applies the symbolic information to her waking life. She receives insights from within and discovers that she can make her own decisions. With this new tool she begins to explore her individuality, taking risks to achieve goals she thinks are important. She discovers her personal power and a hero is born.

NEXT, THE HERO begins a meditation practice and meets the Magician in herself. She begins to realize she has a divine nature. In her budding awareness she comes to see herself as a unique and magnificent being possessing magical talents. Like the magician on the card she learns to access a higher part of herself. In doing so she begins to bring her gifts into the world.

EVENTUALLY, USING PRAYER and meditation, the hero taps into the archetype of the High Priestess, which leads her to reassess her spiritual values. Diving into her inner sanctum she reorganizes her own philosophy, emerging as a person of high moral integrity who serves as her own counsel. Her awareness opens up and she begins to make choices based upon the spiritual good of all.

IN ORDER TO KNOW her authentic self, she must now come to terms with her inner parents, The Empress and Emperor. Once her

## Messages from the Archetypes

personality traits and second hand values received from her parents and culture have been assessed, she chooses which ones to keep and which ones to throw away. The hero grows into her authentic adult self and learns to access, within herself, the nurturing female energy of the Empress and the assertive male energy of the Emperor.

BY NOW THE HERO has grown considerably. Much of her inner work is done and she has learned about the world through mentors and books. Thus she becomes a teacher herself, symbolized by the Hierophant. She now knows what is true and can bring her wisdom to others.

DURING THE JOURNEY the hero is often faced with choices of the heart, symbolized by the Lovers. She learns that her choices must be made, in part, by taking others' feelings into consideration. The art of loyalty and commitment to friends and family teach her about love.

WHEN FACED WITH the many challenges in the world, the hero finds herself meeting those challenges by taking on important missions. She is an active participant in the world and assertively rides the Chariot over any difficulties in her path.

# Using Tarot for Healing and Spiritual Growth

She likes riding the crest of success, and making positive changes for herself.

LIVING HER LIFE authentically requires that she get in touch with her basic animal instincts. She discovers her animal self is strong, with a mind of its own. The world is full of delicacies for the body, or the animal self. Unhealthy but good tasting food, sexual attractions and the like provide many temptations and opportunities for her to exercise Strength over her animal impulses.

SOMETIMES THE HERO must retreat from the world and turn inward. As the Hermit archetype symbolizes, she chooses to spend part of every day in quiet contemplation. She meditates upon circumstances and significant others in her life. By and by, an understanding arises about their roles in her journey towards self-awareness and self-development.

IN HER LIFE THE HERO must come to accept crisis and loss. She realizes that when fate, as symbolized by the Wheel of Fortune, turns in her favor she succeeds at what she is attempting to do; when it turns the other way, she fails.

FAILURE LEADS THE HERO to acquire the objectivity of her fair witnessing mind, symbolized by the Justice card. Because she can view her life from a larger perspective, mistakes become her teachers. In the process, she begins to weigh and measure her intentions and desires with a projected outcome.

## MESSAGES FROM THE ARCHETYPES

This learned, she becomes adept at discerning right from wrong action.

AT TIMES, THE HERO needs to make significant changes in her life but she may feel like the Hanged Man unable to make a decision and suspended in her actions. Time passes and a new perspective emerges; she experiences an insight and knows just what to do.

THE HERO THEN makes a decision. In this case, Death symbolizes the grim reaper archetype within. He sweeps his sickle and cuts away the limited thinking that put her into emotional crisis and kept her from growing. When the change is made, maturation continues.

THE ANGEL OF TEMPERANCE depicts the hero's confidence and emotional calm during the crisis periods and eventual changes. She finds a place in herself that transcends and embraces both the positive and negative aspects of life. She learns self-acceptance.

SOME CHANGES REQUIRE the hero to journey to the underworld of her psyche. There she discovers what is responsible for her mental and emotional discomfort. She dialogues with the Devil, a shadowy archetype, who teaches by causing trouble. Like the couple depicted on the card, she comes to see how she chains herself to outdated modes of thinking.

WITH DECISIVE ACTION, the hero then makes changes in the way she thinks. She awakens to the false beliefs and artificial conditioning in her culture and in herself. The Tower that was constructed by her old ways of thinking is now torn down.

AFTER THE HERO'S struggles with the dark forces, she goes on to encounter within herself the archetypal principle of the Star. She discovers a part of herself through which Spirit or God can help her serve others. She begins to live not according to her own will, but relaxes into the creative flow of her spiritual nature and allows it to lead her.

THE HERO THEN comes under the influence of the Moon archetype, which is the feminine principle. It teaches her to make choices based upon an authentic part of herself that is in harmony with the Now. Thus she overcomes illusion and easily recognizes concepts that are foreign to her feminine nature.

THE SUN, OR the masculine principle in her personality, grows strong and triumphs over any dark forces that threaten to hold her back from her journey. She learns to live contentedly with others becoming a flexible and effective member of a team. She cooperates in shared visions that make a difference in the world.

THE HERO IS NOW able to make good Judgments that enable her to live according to higher principles. Now, possessing compassion for herself and others and an unwavering faith she gives birth to a more complete self.

THE HERO SELF-ACTUALIZES into a happy and healthy person. She has realized, accepted and integrated the higher and lower archetypal parts of herself.

In the process, she discovers her authentic self and knows she is a child of the universe, symbolized by the World.

As you can see, the tradition of Tarot represents psychological energies inherent in the human species. In other decks, for example Tavaglione's Stairs of Gold, the cards contain the symbols of the Hebrew alphabet, of astrology and of numerology, which give even more archetypal information to the advanced practitioner of Tarot.

## A Brief History of Tarot

TAROT fIRST APPEARED in Europe as the familiar deck of playing cards in the early 1400s. The earliest known cards with images are the fifteenth century Italian Visconti-Sforza deck. The link to the Visconti-Sforza family is based upon family emblems that are found on the cards.

For centuries the symbolism on these cards has intrigued occultists, artists and art historians, especially since they have been preserved and reproduced on Tarot decks for over 500 years often with additional personal artistic touches based upon the important topics, fashions, and events of their time. Many of these decks are on display at leading museums and libraries throughout the world.

## Using Tarot for Healing and Spiritual Growth

Painters like Pamela Coleman Smith of the Rider-Waite deck and Lady Frieda Harris of the Aleister Crowley deck, were among the talented people who helped develop the Tarot symbolism we know today.

Some researchers speculate that Tarot was first used as a philosophy for promoting conscious psychological change. But in the fifteenth and sixteenth centuries, Tarot was primarily known as a fortune telling device. Since the game was also associated with gambling it was outlawed in many cities. For the esoteric philosophers it would make sense to keep their practices secret, since the Church viewed such activities with suspicion.

During the thirteenth century, the Church had successfully established a dogmatic theology, and argument from philosophers or anyone else who dared to be different was met with imprisonment, exile or death. In this way the early Church rooted out heresies against their religion. Under the Church's influence hundreds of philosophers, mystics and healers were persecuted. As the church's authority became more rigidly established, mainstream philosophies gradually moved underground and the scope of higher reasoning became narrower.

In order to communicate their esoteric ideas to each other these "heretics" modified the Tarot imagery to include their philosophical ideas and beliefs creating a pictorial language rich in archetypal symbolism and specialized symbols. Thus the mysteries could be secretly and safely revealed to others who understood the symbolic language of the soul, or as psychologists would say, the unconscious mind. A system of evocative emblems evolved, gradually becoming more complex.

The narrow medieval mind-set began to decline during the fourteenth century. The weakening of the church continued and by the sixteenth and seventeenth centuries esoteric groups began to spread throughout Europe, Britain and eventually America. Certain French esoteric lodges, (connected with the Masonic orders) considered Tarot a serious and worthy study. They wrote volumes and kept this mystical paradigm alive. As a result of this inheritance, many people are now discovering how to use Tarot as a tool for self-development.

In her book, *The Underground Stream*, Tarot scholar Christine Payne Towler writes:

> The fact that the Tarot tradition has survived this many years is nothing short of a miracle: having outlived the tyranny of the early religionists as well as some very hardheaded secular leaders, Tarot must command respect for that alone. Generations of souls lived and died for these images so that you might have them to contemplate and meditate upon in this century. We do not want to be guilty of taking this hard won legacy from the philosophers of antiquity for granted!

Today, there is a resurgence of interest in Tarot. Authentically reproduced Tarot decks and highly creative contemporary versions are available in every major bookstore, with literally hundreds of styles from which to choose. You can buy decks relating to Celtic Shamanism, Native American spirituality, Shakespeare and abstract art.

It is not uncommon to run across mention of this old card game in a novel or magazine article, indeed, there is even a Tarot reader in Deepak Chopra's novel *Merlin*. A poem by T. S. Eliot, *The Waste Land*, mentions the cards. A library in New England once issued its annual report on the backs of oversized Tarot cards, and a large bank used them in a 30 second television commercial as a metaphor for making money grow. Tarot designs now appear on fabric, greeting cards, games, paintings, jewelry, key chains and on a variety of arts and crafts. Tarot, it seems, is woven into the fabric of our modern-day lives.

However, fear, suspicion and superstition continue and some clients may feel uncomfortable with the use of Tarot cards in counseling. One day, a young client walked past my desk and picked up a Tarot card from my table. She exclaimed appreciatively "Oh, what a beautiful picture." I told her it was a Tarot card.

She immediately closed her eyes and turned her face sharply away from the picture. She dropped the card as she told me that her church would not allow her to look at Tarot cards.

Many Christian religions continue to warn their congregation about the use of these decks, for they see Tarot as something unholy, even demonic. It is not wise to engage people who have dark thoughts and feelings about them because, due to their own thinking, they might see the messages coming forth as evil.

But for those who search for innovative answers to life's issues, Tarot can speak with a marvelous eloquence to seekers who question them wisely. For many of my clients, the science and art of this old, powerful system has proven to be profoundly enlightening.

Chapter Four

# Conscious Archetypal Energy and Healing

*I Am Love*

**My introduction** to archetypal energy was a mystical one. It was a profound encounter that occurred in my twenties, and because of that experience —and a gauntlet of life's teachings in the years that followed—I see the world, and myself in a more comprehensive and holistic way.

At twenty-eight my spirituality was maturing. I could see that everything was too beautiful, too complex and too well designed to be accidental. I sincerely wanted to know more about the creator of the world in which I lived.

Staying open to all possibilities, I prayed, "Who are you that has made this place?"

I didn't get an answer right away so I asked and asked and asked for I was determined to receive an answer. (The world is so distracting that this kind of intensity in prayer is not easy.) I waited. I read. I sewed and I cooked. I took care of my children, meditated, practiced yoga, ate healthy food, and listened to music. All the while, I searched with my senses. Still, there was no response.

After about a month of continually asking, "Who are you?" an answer finally came. Suddenly I felt a loving and compassionate presence, much like a softly flowing river. I immediately knew this was the spiritual answer that I had been asking for because it was more intensely loving than anything I had felt in ordinary life. The Spirit's flowing unconditional love and deep compassion gently encapsulated my body. It ran through my heart center at the middle of my chest while it caressed my cheek like a gentle summer's breeze.

The experience was multi-sensory. Without words the Spirit telepathically communed. It was aware of me, loved me and had compassion for my struggles. At the same time, I heard a sound much like a choir of angelic sopranos holding a steady note —a feminine "Auuuumm." At the time, I knew nothing of the Aum sound or its origins. I later learned of its use in Buddhism and other oriental meditative practices. Buddhism like many patriarchal religions is based upon men's experiences. The Aum, often heard in the meditative traditions, is of a masculine tone but mine was feminine.

The experience lasted for about a minute. It communicated not in words, but with a felt knowing that "It" was what I called "God." It needed neither name nor gender and had neither beginning nor end. My intelligence seemed small compared to the intelligence of this Spirit and I knew I did not have the capacity to know It completely.

Because of this mystical communion I have come to know our creator as an intelligent and conscious energy, the archetypal pattern of a loving Spirit.

Since that time, I have spent many hours exploring how to tap into this archetypal energy at various levels of consciousness. The exploration of dreams, imagery and meditation are internal techniques that bridge unconscious information with the ego, Whereas Tarot and other forms of art expression are external techniques. The symbolic and synchronistic magic I have observed while using these healing tools has changed my culturally conditioned ideas of materialistic separateness from God to a more inclusive vision. I see and feel an energetically connected world.

The body contains conscious energy, and this energy flows

through the body much like a river, complete with multiple Chakras or points of energy concentration. We move this energy with our thinking and our intention. It is replete with archetypal patterns of information that we can access depending upon our level of consciousness, affect, body postures, facial expression and—even the clothes we wear. I see this spiritual world through my inner vision and feel it with my energy body. To me, this spiritual world is a reality that has become an intrinsic part of my practice. I believe that every person has a similar spiritual core, and that each of us can tap into that Spirit to enhance our work and lives.

Throughout history many people have explored this energy of consciousness and attempted to map and diagram it for others. Sigmund Freud, for example, identified various levels of the human consciousness: the id, ego, super conscious, preconscious and the unconscious. Both he and Carl Jung thought that the mind's consciousness contained levels of information about who we are personally and collectively and that we could access this information through logical thinking and intuitive insights.

When working with Tarot, the images we see tap into archetypal levels of consciousness within us. The questioner first views the image on the card allowing his or her memories to rise to consciousness. I encourage them to free associate. When the person has no more to say, I offer an intuitive interpretation of the card. This interpretation also taps into a place in their consciousness where they know the truth of a situation. When this happens insights burst forth in a wellspring of answers for the questioner.

Twenty-eight-year-old Melissa sought wellness counseling due to two physical ailments: chronic constipation and vaginal irritation. She was scheduled to see a traditional physician and decided to make an appointment with me to explore her body's wisdom. Her life was in constant flux. Melissa worked odd jobs, traveling around the state and abroad. She had a partner but it was a sexual paring, each going their separate ways after a once-a-week get-together.

Because of the location of her symptoms we discussed her body issues as they related to the first two Chakras. The first Chakra has to do with sex and other survival of the species issues. The second Chakra deals with reproduction, but also contains stored information about the culture and the family of origin. At the physical level I taught her about how depression can slow the bowels causing constipation.

We then turned to the Tarot cards. Melissa chose the Voyager Tarot deck. The faces of the cards in this deck have photographic collages depicting modern life. Clients easily identify with the symbolism. She asked the question, " What do I need to know to help me with my health issues?"

The first card, of a four-card spread, was entitled "Regenerator and Sage of Cups." Melissa said "I see a couple of men tending the earth by pouring water on it. This seems to be addressing my need for nurturance. The two older people in the corner of the card seems like wise counselors." I also saw this card as a reflection of her seeking wise counsel and nurturing, thus supporting her intuitive process.

The second card, entitled "Empress," evoked a strong emotional reaction. "She is spiritually evolved and in tune with all of nature," Melissa said with awe. The card's image was of a golden woman standing proudly in a field of flowers, a snow-topped volcano appeared in the background and a beautiful waterfall was at her side. An image of the earth with its swirling weather patterns was behind her and a multi pedaled flower fanned out around her head like a large dramatic crown. To finish the spiritual scene a white dove of peace flew above it all.

I knew Melissa's consciousness was tapping into, and feeling, the archetypal energy of the Empress. I asked Melissa to describe where in her body she was feeling the feminine energy. She thought for a moment then, with a sweeping gesture of her hand, she indicated her heart and lower abdomen saying "I feel the Empress's energy at my heart Chakra and then all the way down my body."

Melissa's reaction to the Empress archetype included the area of her body that was symptomatic. I thought Melissa would benefit by exploring this image at a deeper level of consciousness. The spontaneous imagery or visualization found at the preconscious level of the self can uncover insights and wisdom beyond the knowing of the conscious ego. I discussed this with her and she agreed to use a visualization technique to explore the Empress archetype. I had her close her eyes, and then led her through a brief relaxation phase (described in chapter one). Next, I asked her to allow an image of the Empress to form in her imagination. After a brief pause, Melissa reported she saw the Empress in a quiet forest meadow.

With her eyes still closed, Melissa described the Empress as dressed in a flowing white gown and different from the image on the card. She then internally dialogued with the Empress. The image said, " I am the Empress, the feminine spirit of nature, animals and humankind. I am here to assist you in your healing."

Next, I told Melissa to become the Empress, in her imagination. After a brief quiet meditation in which Melissa embodied the archetype, I asked her to describe her experience. Her affect and voice softened as she talked about ways to live in harmony and "making every step sacred in honor of the earth and all its inhabitants."

As the imagery session came to a close, the Empress told Melissa that she would be available to her anytime she needed advice or support. Melissa need only to close her eyes with the intention of contacting her and she would be there. When she felt done, I asked her to return to waking consciousness where upon we continued the discussion about how to walk life's path with the integrity and grace of the Empress.

The third card, entitled "Lovers" is the archetype of relationships. She looked at this card for what seemed like a long time. "What's happening for you?" I asked. She said, "There are two people in an embrace on the card." Her voice began to trail away as she mentioned some other aspects in a rather superficial way. I then asked her if she wanted to visualize this card too. She issued a sharp "no!" With this response I decided whatever messages she was getting from this card was very personal and she wasn't ready to discuss them with me. I respected this and gave her space by talking about the card's interpretation. I told her "The symbol of the lovers represents different kinds of love and the choices love calls upon us to make. The Empress makes choices based upon integrity and is true to herself and honest in her relationships."

I intuitively put forth a hunch, I said, "Maybe the Empress is calling upon you to *make every step a sacred step* in your relationships too." Melissa closed her eyes, let out a long sigh and said, "That is just what I needed to hear."

We didn't discuss Melissa's love life. Instead we focused on the wisdom she needed to begin making better choices for herself. I took this receptive time to suggest, "Maybe you wouldn't have vaginal problems if you align your heart and your actions in your relationships," She softly looked me in the eye and nodded yes.

The fourth card was entitled "Guardian and Woman of Crystals." The card shows a woman surrounded by multi faceted crystals, with one on her forehead. This is the archetype of intuitive and intellectual mastery. This card prompted a discussion around getting out of the head or intellect and listening to the body's wis-

**Guardian Woman of Crystals**

dom. In my assessment, she was so bombarded with parental, cultural, and commercial values that her ability to "look within for answers" was limited.

Lastly, I began to teach Melissa how to notice valuable innate intuitive impulses and translate them through the equally valuable intellect.

As you can see, when the questioner looks at the cards it is like looking into a mirror. In the card-mirror, symbols cause thoughts and feelings to bubble up from the preconscious and unconscious mind. With the guidance of a trained Tarot counselor, the archetypal energy of the symbols leads the questioner to deep insights necessary for self-development and self-acceptance.

In my experience of Tarot, something happens beyond our everyday awareness to affect the performance of the cards. As in the example of Melissa, the thinking and feeling states of the client synchronistically affect the order of the cards as they are shuffled and placed into a predetermined formation. The layout of the images reflected the psychological profile of Melissa's question.

Synchronicity, which can be viewed as part of our conscious energy structure, manifests itself in the form of seemingly coincidental occurrences, which symbolically connect our psyches to the events that are happening in the world. Because this does not make logical sense, synchronicity is often experienced as a miracle, serendipity or pure chance.

Synchronistic events disrupt our everyday notions of reality, thus giving us a larger sense of the world in which we live. Indeed, such experiences—which the mystics write about—suggest that there is a direct interaction between the material world and our feelings, behaviors and thoughts. Working with Tarot, Dreams and guided imagery often brings us closer to this mystical realm of experience, one that always enriches the healing potential within.

# Using Tarot for Healing and Spiritual Growth

**The Case of Maria**

My heart felt open and loving as I prepared to act as a conduit for healing energy. I could feel the warm energy flowing through my hands; I placed one hand on Maria's left shoulder, and the other near her heart. Maria, who was sitting in a chair, complained of a limited range of motion in her left arm, a condition she referred to as "frozen shoulder." "I can't sleep more than two hours a night. I wake up in pain after the medication wears off."

Her mother was slowly dying of a liver ailment. Maria was expressing confused emotions and a desire to run away. I knew her mind was sending quantum waves of emotion throughout her body, especially in the area of her heart and throat Chakras. The area in her shoulder was responding dramatically, and painfully. I believed that her confused and grieving heart was reflected in the incapacitated shoulder. I also felt she had many parental issues to work through—to express, accept and forgive.

"Your hands are really hot!" Maria exclaimed, closing her eyes and settling into a meditative state. As her waking consciousness melted into a more receptive level, her body became more permeable to the intelligent healing consciousness being directed by my intention and the laying on of hands.

I explained to Maria that as long as this energy is flowing smoothly in your body, your senses, organs and systems function optimally. Stress diminishes this life force, and a person may eventually become diseased or, as in the case of Maria, weakened and subject to injury.

In my experience, the energy through my hands stops and flows as needed by the client. It decreases inflamed tissues and alleviates pain. Sometimes the effects of hands on healing last a couple of hours, and sometimes the condition is healed. That night, Maria slept through the night for the first time in months.

Since my experience with the archetypal spiritual energy, I have read extensively. I have found that others have felt the same Spirit. The world's religions contain references to it in their traditions and now scientists are validating this ancient energy in the laboratory.

When researchers examine the effects of this energy they report consistent and remarkable results, and some scientists postulate that we do seem to be a part of something greater than ourselves and in participation with a consciousness beyond ourselves. The words flow and river are often associated with this formless and genderless quantum field of energy.

Essentially, I see the entire world as energetic and conscious. The world is manifested by an intelligent life force or flow of energy that makes up the human form, animals, plants and inanimate objects such as rocks. A similar idea is known in virtually every traditional culture throughout the world. Whether it be Native American, Greek, African, Japanese or Chinese, a life energy is recognized as an entity unto itself that resides in physical objects. This energetic life force is often described as being like a river with no beginning and no end and is known by various names: Chi, Pneuma, Prana, Qi, Flow, or Spirit.

Whatever the name or the description, it is still the same life force, a flowing creative energy of the universe. We are It. It surrounds and permeates and *is* every sense, organ and cell. How much we realize and honor that we are spiritual energy affects our physical, psychological and spiritual health.

This consciousness is an energetic, or spiritual, part of us, a continuation of the outer waking consciousness inwards toward deeper inner levels and outwardly towards a harmonious unity and a cooperative participation in the world.

Before one can really know one's self and others, one must first gain awareness of an essential inner energetic self, which includes our personal story in images. The inner self contains levels of conscious energy from which springs the imagery of our nighttime dreams, guided imagery, meditation, and our fantasies. This same energy is involved during the intention, questioning, and the layout of the Tarot cards in counseling. One can think of this consciousness as being like the light energy behind a movie projector. The movie or the images are one's personal story available in the psyche in symbolic and mythic terms. The light of the projector is the consciousness energy that combines with the psychological information in the images.

We cannot know the Spirit of conscious energy completely. What we can know becomes apparent to us as subtle and not so subtle clues. It's structure reveals itself in our experiences at the material level. Some people experience these clues.

Carl Jung wrote of a river of consciousness that contains information of the past, present and future. He called this flow the collective unconscious. He said we have a connection to all the information that has been, is and will be. One of the things this means is that we can know future events.

Our dreams bridge the information in the unconscious mind with the conscious ego. For some, it also bridges the collective unconscious with the conscious ego. Because I am so aware of my dreams, I often dream of events that have yet to take place. Once on a camping trip with my daughter Beth and her partner Tommy I had a precognitive dream.

One morning, Tommy told me that he had lost his wallet the day before. I said to him, "That's interesting, because last night, I dreamt of a wallet in water." I told him, "The wallet was sinking in the water and I reached to get it." Tommy replied, "No, I know I took my wallet out of my pants before I got into the boat, so it couldn't have fallen in the water."

Two hours later, the lost and found at the store near the lake contacted Tommy that his wallet had been found. They told him a woman had seen the wallet floating on the water and had reached to get it out before it sank. Tommy found this "too weird" to comprehend. He stayed away from me for the rest of the trip.

Many Tarot layouts have a space for a card that is labeled *future*, but it is impossible to accurately predict what will come. Rather, when this issue comes up in a reading—for example, some clients will want to inquire about a future outcome or direction— I look at the information presented in the cards as one of many potential outcomes. Also, this provides an opportunity to understand how a client feels about his or her future. Is she optimistic or pessimistic? Does he have unrealistic expectations or does he shy away from reaching for his potential.

Over the years I have learned that we unconsciously shape our future, unaware of the attitudes and beliefs that may limit our direction and choices. By bringing these thoughts into consciousness, we gain more control over our lives. Such meditations encourage us to lucidly explore our inner being, tapping into the invisible and spiritual parts of ourselves. For me, this awareness and perspective is a constant reminder to make every step through life a sacred step.

# Section Two

# Working with the Archetypes

Chapter Five

# Getting Started with Tarot

*I Am student*

ALTHOUGH EACH TAROT card contains archetypal meanings that are recognizable by all, each person will find meanings that relate to uniquely to him or her. It is important to develop your intuitive talents, rather than depending upon the interpretations that Tarot books or other readers give.

At the foundation of Tarot counseling is the ability to recognize yourself in the archetypes. Only when you begin to identify archetypal patterns and their possible consequences in your own life can you hope to counsel others. The following techniques will help you become familiar with them.

### Self-Identification Using Tarot

It might be helpful to think of the archetypes as inner guides in your journey of self-discovery. They exemplify a way of being in the world and they are expressed through our personalities. We find archetypal symbols in our imagination, in our dreams and fantasies, and in the world of art, myth, legend, literature and religion.

We experience the archetypes according to our own perspective. For example, spiritual seekers may encounter saints, gods and goddesses while academics and other rationalists may conceive of the archetypes as the invisible patterns in the mind that control how we experience the world. Scientists however, may see archetypes as holographic impressions of the universe. Scholars of psychology study archetypes by examining their presence in art, and literature, comparing them to similar imagery that has existed throughout time.

Each archetype expresses itself on many different levels and is dependent upon the physical, cognitive, emotional and spiritual development of the individual ego. These levels will be explored in greater detail in Section Three.

### Choosing a Personal Deck

I recommend beginning your study of Tarot with the classic Rider-Waite deck. It contains a wealth of symbolic imagery. It is an excellent beginner deck because many contemporary decks are fashioned using its symbols. At the end of this chapter is a summary of traditional meanings for each of the seventy-eight cards.

When choosing a personal Tarot deck, look for imagery that feels right to you. Imagery is the primary language of the preconscious and unconscious mind; the more you resonate with the imagery of the deck, the more the cards will trigger insights.

The imagery on the cards is derived from many sources, including numerology, colorology, astrology and the Hebrew alphabet. The creator of each deck artistically expresses a personal perspective, and you will find that your intuitive responses will change depending upon which deck you choose.

Look at the imagery of the entire deck and notice how it makes you feel. What are the themes that come up for you? If you are attracted to the imagery, if you feel a certain excitement, then it is probably a deck you should have. But don't get too hung up looking for the perfect deck. Often a Tarot reader will collect many decks, each one containing a unique combination of archetypal imagery.

### Pitfalls

Contemplation upon the Tarot cards' messages helps you to focus upon the higher potential of your being. However, there are pitfalls in working with the cards, for they might seem to offer magical answers or cause you to become excessively preoccupied with your issues. You can also develop an over-indulgent interest in the unconscious, producing an unhealthy over-analysis of the self. Once, during a difficult emotional crisis, I found myself obsessively looking for answers in the cards. I kept giving myself readings—sometimes three or four a day, including getting up in the middle of the night to ask my questions. This can cause an imbalance because you spend too much time worrying about your issue and neglect of other aspects of your life.

Another danger can be ego inflation—a false sense of power and grandeur. The synchronicity of the layout can astound others and the adoration you get from them can make you feel powerful. Care must be taken so that your ego will not take credit for the benefits that others receive from their sessions. Once before I began my own Tarot counseling practice, I went for a reading by a "psychic" counselor. Near the end of the session, I sat back impressed at the amazing messages I had just received. Then the psychic began to tell my future and said that I would leave my husband by November. I was appalled. Luckily, November came and went uneventfully. This counselor had a false sense of knowing and a dangerously inflated view of her powers, which resulted in a distorted sense that she could accurately predict my future.

Although, the same pitfalls can be found with any tool designed for working with the inner realms, awareness of the dangers makes us less likely to fall into them.

## Finding Yourself in the Cards

Lets begin our study of Tarot by looking through the cards and selecting those images that seem to capture our character and personality. For example, I can identify my personal attributes in every card of the deck. For instance, the Hermit, the fifth card in the Major Arcana, maintains a strong presence in my psyche because it represents my propensity for spending time alone in meditation and contemplation. The Hermit is also a teacher and represents my desire to share what I learn from my practice of inner exploration. In my own life, the High Priestess reminds to be my own counsel. Because she represents my higher self, I am prompted to make choices towards to a spiritual standard. When I draw this card, either I am already operating in the upper levels of the archetype or I need to bring my consciousness to my inner sanctum for contemplation so that I might attain the right relationship to the issue at hand.

Another card that holds deep meaning for me is the Nine of Swords. The Rider-Waite deck depicts a person sitting up in bed holding their face. Nine Swords are horizontally hung on a dark wall. For me, this card often indicates negative thinking, and when it appears, I question myself to see if I am putting up possible mental barriers to the circumstances I am in.

As you journey down the path of self-development, any negative thinking standing between you and your growth will often show up in the cards. Do not be hard on yourself. These normal negative human traits are what Jung called the "shadow." Be courageous, stand your ground, and look at your negative thinking, and emotional mood swings, for there is much to learn from these darker corners of the psyche.

Create a Tarot journal and take notes about your impressions of the cards and their associations to your life. Keep an open mind and do not make judgments, looking at the positive and negative feelings like a scientific investigator taking an inventory.

The system of Tarot is a tool to connect you with your higher levels of mind or wisdom. You will learn that you have more than one vantage point from which to make choices about your thinking, your behavior and your emotions. You will gain self-knowledge and you will help your clients make the same inner connections.

One last important point: all our answers and truths are within. The cards merely provide a point of focus that assists us in accessing our own inner truths.

USING TAROT FOR HEALING AND SPIRITUAL GROWTH

### Layouts for Self Analysis

There are many types of spreads but my three favorite forms are the Daily Card Study, the Daily Direction and the Celtic Cross. The Daily Card Study is an excellent way to attune your self to the power of Tarot and its archetypes. The Daily Direction is specific to the moment and is useful in self-assessment. The third, the Celtic Cross, is one of the oldest layouts and lends itself to many kinds of questions. As you practice giving readings, you will intuitively feel how each spread works.

After choosing a deck and shuffling the cards with an expectation of receiving an answer, the questioner lays them out in a specific pattern, or spread. The result is a segmented pictorial layout of the question and its possible hidden problems and creative solutions.

### Daily Card Study

1. To help you find your own symbolic truths, begin by picking one card from the deck on a daily basis. Write down in your journal whatever comes into your mind, your feelings and your senses. Take your time for you are building personal meanings for each card.

2. How does this image make you *feel*? Where in your body do you feel the card's energy? Name the feelings. They may range from love to irritation, from jealousy to tenderness, from depression to elation. When your feelings are identified, make an association with events from your current life situation. You might also want to identify when in your life have you felt these feelings and under what circumstances. For example, if you were to draw the Magician it might remind you of those times in your life when you felt the most creative.

3. Next, ask yourself, what *desire* or urge towards an activity does the image on the card bring up for you. There may be more than one, such as desire to write or call to a friend, express your feelings, travel, heal or be in nature. How do you experi-

ence this urge or desire in your body? For example, when I look upon the Knight of Swords it reminds me of my desire to write. The Knight holds his sword of the intellect near his head—the part of the body I use as I begin to write.

4. Observe your *thoughts* as you study the card. When one though emerges, notice it and write it down. When another thought comes up, do the same, and so on. If you think you are not having thoughts, realize that this too is a thought. The point is to watch your stream of consciousness as it flows by: opinions, nonsense, arguments, images, memories and body sensations.

5. Notice the *observer*, the part of you that watches your life unfold and observes your sensations, feelings, desires and thoughts. You are that conscious being. Say inwardly: "I am a self, I have a center of pure consciousness." Then be quiet and seek to realize this. You may discover that you are not in touch with this part of yourself, for it is not an easy task to integrate the observer into your life. Just keep in mind that this part of you is not missing. It is just a matter of becoming self-aware.

Sometimes you will come face to face with a negative aspect of an archetype, and when this occurs you must approach it with respect. This often happens when the death card appears. Most people see it as a fearful image. When you approach the death card write down all of your thoughts and feelings. Do not reject its negative teachings. You cannot heal anything in yourself that you reject. Learn to see negative aspects like fear and aggressive impulses with a lack of self-judgment. When you are overly judgmental you are not fully accepting of your human nature. Denial and harsh judgment of the lesser side of your nature, or the archetypes, only serves to repress awareness of negative traits. Accepting and integrating the lower levels or shadow aspects of the self is essential to self-actualization of your full potential.

Visualization accesses the preconscious level of imagery of your imagination, and it is here that the archetypes come alive.

Approached with respect, these inner images will help you reach insight and inspiration.

Looking at the card you have picked, cultivate an attitude of curiosity much like Alice in Wonderland. Then close your eyes and calm your mind by focusing your attention upon your breathing. As you move into a meditative state and your thinking slows, down various images and scenes will come into view. Explore these images in your imagination and see what information they bring.

As you access your higher consciousness, in this way, be open to receiving more information. When I do this exercise I sit at a table with a pad and pen readily available. I open my eyes slightly to write down important words or phrases, keys to help me remember when I come out of the meditative state. If I wait until the end of the meditation some of the information will have dropped from my memory (much like dreams disappear from your awareness as you wake up). For example, as I approached my fiftieth birthday I realized I had a fear of aging. During a meditation, I imagined myself sitting in the lap of Jesus, the savior archetype. I was a small child and I rested my head upon his chest. The gentle rhythm in his breath matched my own and lulled me into a feeling of peace and contentment. Inspiration flowed in to me. Still in his lap, I opened my eyes slightly and wrote down "It is not every child that gets to live a long life. Old age is a privilege."

When you feel you have reached a calm meditative place in yourself, a state of relaxed alertness, step into the imaginary land of the card. Take some time to look around at the details. What are the colors and textures of the imaginary place? What sounds are present? Are there any smells? What are the feelings this card provokes? Notice how your body feels in this place. You are then ready to, dialogue with the images.

Unlike fantasy, we do not control this level of imagery. Be open, allowing the images to take on a life of their own. From the higher levels of our consciousness the images bring gifts of insight, clarity and truth. You may want to experiment with the sensation of becoming the image and experience how it feels and thinks. The more open you are to receiving the card's archetypal messages, the more likely it will guide you toward greater meaning in your life.

During exercises such as these, know that you are in complete control. If at any time you are uncomfortable you have only to open your eyes to return to in waking consciousness.

Contemplation upon the Tarot cards' messages helps you to focus on the higher potential of your being. Like Alice, you begin to cultivate wonder and find pleasure in your imaginative dreaming self.

### Daily Direction

This spread provides the questioner a self-portrait of the archetypal energies in your day at the time of the shuffle. You may want

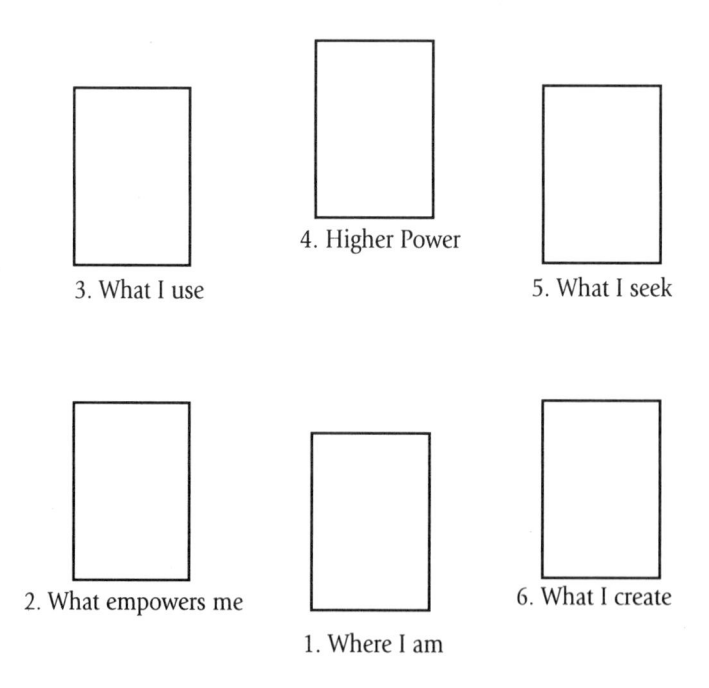

4. Higher Power

3. What I use

5. What I seek

2. What empowers me

1. Where I am

6. What I create

# Using Tarot for Healing and Spiritual Growth

to ask a question simply throw the cards to see what comes up. Look at the spread as a segmented dream image. Like dreams, the images on the cards give you important information about what is going on in your psyche and about the situation in your life today. Listen with both your intellectual mind and intuitive heart and you will learn about your desires, your feelings and your needs.

### Layout Sequence and Sample Interpretation

1. "Where I am," the first position, indicates the major archetype operating in the questioner. For instance, Johnny, a writer, threw the Rider-Waite cards for his daily direction. In this position, the first card we turned up was the Five of Wands. This card shows five young men in an intense struggle. In their hands are five large Wands. He said, "This is what I have been doing today—struggling. Struggling with my family about my mother's estate."

2. "What empowers me" the second position, suggests what influences are needed to inspire movement towards a goal. It indicates something that will help move the situation to completion. Johnny's second card was the Seven of Wands. This card shows a man with a large wand in his hand facing six Wands that stick up, lower than him, from the base of the card. "What empowers me is my creativity." He said, "There is a lot of work to be done. I know what to do but I don't like having to be the only one that does."

3. "What I use," the third position in the spread, reveals thoughts, feelings and behaviors about the issue. The Sun card fell in this place in Johnny's layout and shows a nude child happily riding a white horse. The sun is high in the sky, beneficently radiating over the child. "I am reminded that I have a higher mission," he said. "I need to be writing, revising my manuscript for that television producer. I don't want to have to deal with my family."

4. "Higher Power," the fourth position, refers to the unconscious

strengths that come from the wise part of the questioner. The Emperor turned up in this position of Johnny's spread. Johnny looked at the card, which depicts a bearded man upon a throne with rams' heads adorning it. The man's affect is stern and he has a large crown on his head and wears knight's armor beneath his red robe. Johnny immediately said, " This guy is in a position of power, he knows what to do and he directs things. It dawns on me that this is a part of myself that I often use when I am dealing with other members of my family."

5. "What I seek," the fifth position, helps clarify a goal or vision for the day. In Johnny's layout, the Seven of Swords fell here. This card depicts a man carrying five swords while two are left sticking in the ground. "I wanted to write today," He said. "This image tells me that I didn't get to write like I wanted to."

6. "What I create," the sixth position, shows what the questioner wants to create; the focus of goals to achieve during the day. This card depicts the possibilities and outcome that a person can achieve during the day. The Three of Wands filled this position in Johnny's spread. Johnny looked at the man on the card who was gazing out to sea towards a ship coming in. "This is me, wanting to make plans to rewrite that documentary but I didn't get to it because I felt so bad about what is going on in my family." He paused, and then said, "I'll do it tomorrow. "

## Celtic Cross

Each placement in the Celtic Cross spread gives us information where certain inner and outer influences are occurring concerning a specific situation. (See Celtic Cross spred on page 66).

# Using Tarot for Healing and Spiritual Growth

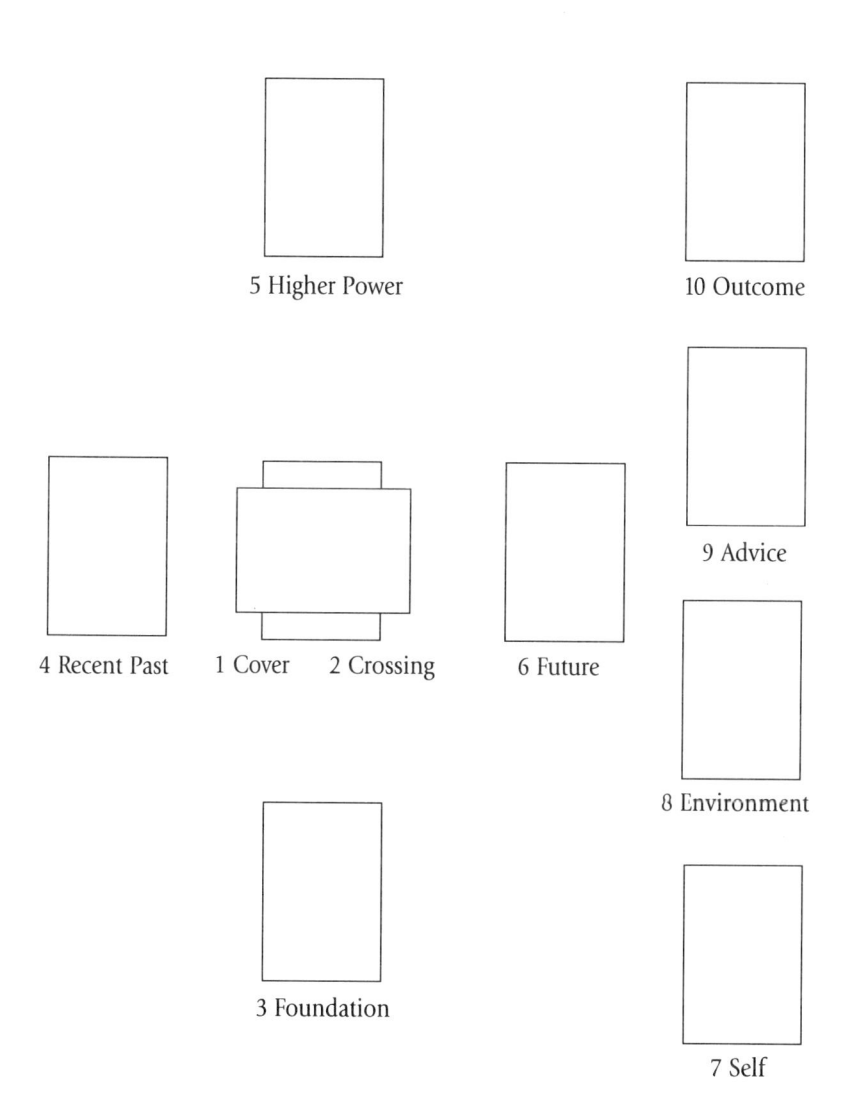

5 Higher Power

10 Outcome

9 Advice

4 Recent Past    1 Cover    2 Crossing    6 Future

8 Environment

3 Foundation

7 Self

## Position Interpretation

1. The Cover card displays the portrait of the basic situation, or central issue.

2. Crossing card joins the cover card to add to the pictorial statement about the concerns of the reading. The crossing card sometimes forms an opposition to the cover card. For instance, the Star, a card of hope, may form an opposition to a more negative card such as the three of Swords. The crossing card can also depict a result that has developed out of the cover card situation. For instance, if the Star is the Cover Card and the three of Swords is crossing, it the person may feel hopeless and depressed about the situation.

3. The Foundation card depicts a root cause of the current situation. It points to a general condition that led to the developments in the first two cards. This card may also reveal a person's early developmental issues. For instance, once in a reading the Lovers card was in this position. This indicated that the questioner was at a crossroads and had some choices to make regarding a relationship. It also indicated that her life's learning gave her the skills necessary to make this choice.

4. The Recent Past card indicates what has been happening recently in regard to the shuffler's question. It may show something that is finished but that still affects the questioner. For example, during a reading the Tower card showed up in this position. The questioner had just been with a friend and they had been discussing ways that the client could change the structure of her relationship.

5. The Over Soul card may reflect the questioner's unconscious or preconscious intuition of where the situation is headed. For instance, the High Priestess in this position may indicate that the questioner is meeting the challenge of the situation by accessing inner spiritual strength and following a higher road to resolution.

6. The Future Influences card describes an influence that is about to enter a person's life. It is an indication of the unconscious currents at work in the present situation. It is not the outcome of the issue but it is part of its unfolding.

7. The Self card gives an indication of what the questioner brings to the situation. It can be an important card in the spread because it gives clues about blocks and inhibitions that are contributing factors to the question or the situation at hand. For instance, the two of Swords in this position may indicate a pessimistic attitude about dealing with others.

8. The Environment card shows influences coming from outside the self. It could be a specific ally or the environment. The ten of cups in this position could indicate an ally who loves the questioner and who is positively disposed towards them.

9. The Hopes and Fears card indicates the person's attitudes and desires, and may be an indication of an issue that needs to be worked through. For instance, the Death card in this position could indicate fear of change. The counseling process could reveal ways to work through this fear.

10. The Outcome or Possibilities card sums up the spread and indicates the most likely outcome given the influences. Never consider this outcome fixed because the reading itself merely shows the way things are proceeding. For instance, the Queen of Wands in this position could indicate that the questioner is in creative control of the situation and would be an inspiration to others.

**Appling the Celtic Cross Layout in a Reading**

One day my friend of many years, Asanté, dropped by my office to visit. He seemed mildly depressed, and like a good friend, I inquired about his dark mood. "I get so tired of the police pulling me over just because I'm a black man," he said. He talked and I listened as he poured out his frustration as he had done so many times before. The bottom line was that here he was again—feeling rejected by his own society. As I have come to understand this issue it is something akin to being rejected by your family.

I didn't know what say that I hadn't already said so I suggested that we consult the cards. Asanté agreed and I decided that the Celtic Cross would give us the best opportunity to explore Asanté's unconscious mind for the answers to this very difficult and challenging racial issue.

Asanté chose the Voyager deck—with its photographic images arranged in collages—and asked the question "How do I find peace with continuing racial injustice in this society?"

The first card or Cover card represents the portrait of the basic situation, or central issue. Asanté had turned up the card called "Integrity" and the Nine of Wands. Integrity represents the archetypal principle of walking your own path with courage and integrity. Among the photos on the collage are: several high towering religious cathedrals, a backbone, large golden genderless statue, white birds flying over the top portion of the card and black hands holding a ceremonial rope.

"This card reminds me of a miracle," Asanté said. When I asked him how this related to his question, he responded, "I see the hands as my need for some wisdom to hang on to and the reflected light on the church gives me hope that I might see more clearly. It almost feels as if a miracle is needed to overcome the obstacles society puts in my way."

The Cover Card and his interpretation told me that Asanté had the courage to ask for help in order to turn his negative thinking towards a wiser perspective.

The second card crosses over the Cover Card to give additional meaning to the central issue of the reading. The Crossing Card was the "Ten of Crystals," and represents the archetypal principle of imagination and pursuing a vision. One image on the card is a bright guiding star shining down upon a night dessert.

"I see focused light," Asanté said pointing to the star in the sky. "It will give me direction to see more clearly."

## Using Tarot for Healing and Spiritual Growth

I saw the focused light as Asanté's honest and serious need to manage this issue. The Crossing card and his interpretation told me he was open to finding direction in the cards.

The third card, the Foundation, represents a root cause of the current situation. It points to a general condition that led to the developments in the first two cards. This card may also reveal a person's early developmental issues.

The card turned up was "Death," number XIII of the Major Arcana and represents the archetypal principle of change and regeneration. Among the images in the Voyager deck are a cloaked human figure, a full moon in the night sky, leaves and a snake shedding its skin. In the middle of the card stands an imposing stone-carved face with staring eyes and a tight-lipped mouth.

"This is rottenness, stale stuff. Racism is old rotten stuff. There's no life or light in it but it still exists in a big way," Asanté said pointing to the big stone face on the card.

I saw racism as the foundation of the question.

We then drew the fourth card, in the position of Recent Past, which indicates what has been happening recently in regard to the shuffler's question. It may show something that is finished but that still affects the questioner.

The Recent Past card was entitled "Devil's Play", numbered XV in the Major Arcana. This card represents the archetypal principle of equal respect for the Divine in good and the Divine in evil. There are multiple images, including fireworks in a night sky, a rather large mushroom and a black man playing a flute. Looming large in the center of the card are two nude gremlin-type characters laughing and living it up like they are at a party.

Asanté immediately said, "The work done by society around race isn't real. There are lots of games and jokes around this issue." Asanté looked sad.

In the Recent Past position I saw his comment and interpretation as representing his entire past, an ongoing negative thinking (albeit an issue of respectable size).

The fifth position stands for the Over Soul card and may reflect the questioner's unconscious intuition of where the situation is now, and where it is headed.

The "Five of Worlds" showed up in the Over Soul position. This card represents the archetypal principle of the growth that takes place because of obstacles. The card's images include five worlds suspended over desert terrain, a forest fire and a dark cornstalk in front of a rainbow coming out of the clouds.

Asanté looked at the card thoughtfully and said, "It reminds me of a journey over rough terrain. I would have a difficult time telling which way to go." He then pointed to the tiny rainbow in the background of the card and said, "I am trying to figure out which way to go. Maybe I should go beyond the rainbow. Maybe there is a better course to take around the racial question. There never seems to be an obvious road to take."

His interpretation told me that his Over Soul or higher consciousness was searching for answers and was hopeful of finding a better perspective.

The sixth position is called Future Influences. In this position, the card's image describes an influence that is about to enter a person's life, an indication of the unconscious currents at work in the present situation. It is not the outcome of the issue but part of its unfolding.

The Ace of Wands turned up, representing the archetypal principle of enlightenment—a way of living that is paved with truth and that leads you to live your life to the fullest. In the Voyager deck the image contains multiple-strips of photographic imagery radiating from the center. Superimposed over the center is a hand with a colorful psychedelic x-ray view of the bones. Fireworks seem to be flying from the tips of the fingers.

Asanté said, "This is my power to create. It reminds me that I am a powerful influence to those around me. I can create good or I can create in a destructive way. This card is telling me to use that power to influence a society and the racial issues of our time." Since Asanté was our community's advocate for black equal rights this made sense. I knew he had the potential to produce much-needed changes in our society.

The card in the seventh position is simply called "Self" and gives an indication of the questioner's blocks and inhibitions. Asanté turned up "Stagnation" the Eight of Cups. This card represents the archetypal principle of germinating ideas while immersed in a dark mood. In the Voyager deck this is depicted through images of broken pottery and by the water and light in the upper portion of the card. There is also a beautiful green pot with beautiful but aging white flowers.

Asanté noticed a pile of glass shards in the card and said, "This reminds me of the junk at the end of a stream. Sometimes, like our elders, there is something useful in old things."

How does this relate to your question? I asked,

He replied, "There may be answers in our peoples' stories. You know, the ignored wisdom of our elders that is still available. How did they cope with issues of race?" He queried himself. "The last generation of African Americans had it worse and they were kept from the larger culture by segregation." Asanté sat back and looked at me with a furrowed brow, saying, "That doesn't work for me. I can't just sit back and take the abuse."

Since this was the Self-card I felt that his depressed mood was represented well by this card. Yet I saw that he was rapidly moving to a resolution, with very little feedback from me.

The eighth position is called Environment and shows influences coming from outside the self. It could represent a specific friend or factors in the environment.

The "Empress" card, number III of the Major Arcana, was turned up. This card symbolizes the archetypal feminine principle of a nurturing receptivity to all of life. She creates and protects everyone and everything.

Asanté had a quick answer. " You, and women like you are my most powerful and supportive friends." I reminded him that he also had his own share of this feminine archetypal energy. He lowered his eyes and said, " Yes, I got it from my grand-momma."

Asanté and I have been best friends for almost twenty years

and it was a pleasure to share my tools with him, helping him to trust more deeply in his intuitive powers and gifts.

The eighth position, labeled Advice, indicates the person's attitudes, desires, hopes and fears in relation to the issue. This is where the counselor's advice often comes into play.

The card that showed up was entitled "Negativity," Five of Crystals representing the culturally conditioned negative states of one's mind. The images include a hodgepodge of red and black crystals of various shapes.

Asanté looked at the card and, putting his hand on his head, began to free associate, "Broken. No light gets out." He paused thoughtfully then said, "This card makes me think about how you feel when your whole life is consumed with a hate-them-back kind of attitude. My father was like that, and he died a broken angry man. He was never able to accept racial discrimination."

Asanté sat back in his chair, looked at me and said, "If you are not accepted in this society you have to define your own measurement for your success. People who see themselves as successful, even though they may have little money, are often a spiritually strong people."

By talking through his issues with a friend, Asanté drew forth an inner truth. He was being his own counsel and receiving his own inner advice.

The tenth and last card is the Outcome or Possibilities that sum up the spread. It indicates the most likely outcome given the influences and shows the way things are proceeding.

Asanté's last card was "Sorrow," the Six of Cups and symbolizes purification and catharsis that sorrow can evoke. The card's dark images show water scenes and broken Cups. In the center is an upside-down luminous vase pouring beautiful lavender flowers that seem to light up the scene.

"There's always going to be some sadness and anger when you're treated this way by your own country, Asanté reflected. "This kind of pain is a long-standing reality for black folks in America. We must accept that this is true and allow ourselves to feel sad, maybe even cry, to release the negative energy inside. Then we can begin to work with others to change the racial climate of society."

I knew Asanté had a strong belief in his own humanity. He had strong family ties that included elders that demonstrated dignity in living. He had studied black history, benefiting from the legacy left by generations of African Americans. Because of this heritage, Asanté could express his actions in a more positive and constructive way.

## Raising Intuitive Awareness

When I read cards, I always help my clients access their own intuitive wisdom. Only if it is needed will I give an interpretation. For example, one afternoon Trudy stopped by for a Tarot reading. "Who am I?" she asked of the cards. She turned over the Fool, the first card of the Major Arcana. In the deck Trudy chose, the smiling fool has stepped off a cliff and appears suspended in mid-air. He is reaching out for a rose. I had Trudy hold the card in her hand and asked her what she saw.

" The person looks happy as he steps off the cliff," she said. To her, this card represented her willingness to let go of control, "to go with the flow," as she put it.

When Trudy was finished I added the traditional interpretation of the card, which to her delight matched her own. "The fool personifies the spirit of enthusiasm and an openness to a broad range of possibilities when setting forth upon a new adventures," I said. "He has let go of his need for control."

Other Tarot readers rely upon their own intuition, while I focus on the intuitions provided by the client. Both ways work.

## Choosing a Mentor

There is no one right way of practicing Tarot counseling. Those who endeavor to work with this healing art develop according to their own mental and intuitive capacities. However, when you first approach this ancient system of cards it is wise to seek tutoring from an experienced mentor. Learn the teacher's ways and adapt them to complement your capabilities. Since Tarot is a powerful tool, it is important to choose a mentor with moral integrity and spiritual values close to your own.

In my search for a mentor, one of the things I looked for was a person who did not claim to know what was best for me. I wanted someone to assist me in finding my own answers through the counseling process, and it was especially important that my mentor not try to read my future in the cards. I do not consider Tarot to be a future-telling tool. Although prediction may be entirely possible, I have never seen it done with any degree of accuracy. In transpersonal counseling, it may even serve to confuse the client's present issues.

Your potential mentor should possess the ability for thinking symbolically. The mentor should be in touch with his or her intuition and demonstrate a familiarity with the archetypes. If such a person is not immediately available, you may begin with the information I have provided in this chapter.

## Traditional Meanings of the Major Arcana

The Rider-Waite deck contains seventy-eight cards: twenty-two known as the Major Arcana and forty are known as the Minor Arcana including sixteen court cards, similar to the jack, queen and king of a standard deck of playing cards. These cards symbolically represent universal principles and the archetypal energy we experience at different times in our lives. The cards help give structure to the archetypal forces operating through us. You can use the following information to enrich the personal meanings you attributed to the cards in the previous exercises and layouts.

The Major Arcana cards represent broad archetypal themes that give information and guidance on the seeker's psychological and spiritual state. The forty Minor Arcana cards add practical detail to the Major Arcana, and provide additional information on relationships, creative potentials, and the successes and struggles we experience in life.

The court cards of the Minor Arcana are the pages, knights, kings and queens. They can symbolize a particular type of person entering the seeker's life, an aspect of the seeker's personality, or they could indicate a particular event in the person's past or future.

In the Minor Arcana there are four suits—Cups, Wands, Swords, and Pentacles— that represent human conditions. The suit of Cups represents emotions. The suit of Wands represents the active sensations of will, passion, creativity and intuition. The suit of Swords represents the mind or intellect, and the suit of Pentacles represents the body or the material world.

## THE MAJOR ARCANA

The following is a brief summary of the traditional archetypal meanings for the twenty-two cards of the Major Arcana, based upon the imagery of the Rider-Waite deck and other decks with similar pictorial designs.

### 0 ~ The Fool

The fool represents a relative state of non-being, no fear, a free-floating letting go. This archetype refers to the initial impulse that begins the creative flow in new endeavors. It also shows one's feelings at the beginning of a journey: a sense of adventure, wonder and anticipation. The fool symbolizes a person who is open to the mystical, transcendent and transpersonal realms of consciousness.

### I ~ The Magician

The Magician represents well-timed communication and confident well-directed will. It symbolizes someone who is open to the will of Spirit, a will that is directed through him or her and manifests as wise counseling and conduct. One may see this will as coming from the invisible realms of our consciousness, manifested synchronistically in the world.

### II ~ The High Priestess

The high priestess is an androgynous archetype that represents the universal principle of intuition, independence, self-trust and self-resourcefulness. She has balanced yin (soft and receptive) and yang (strong, dynamic assertiveness) energies. Mythically she represents the inner journey or the return to one's self. She has superior wisdom, intelligence and spiritual insight.

### III ~ The Empress

The Empress represents humankind's ability to extend love and to receive love— the ability to extend one's self for the purpose of nurturing one's own or another's growth. The symbol of feminine productivity in action is often represented as Venus, the goddess of love. In Jungian psychology she represents the anima or the feminine principle. She approaches life with an attitude of love and a trusting heart.

### IV ~ The Emperor

The Emperor archetype symbolizes power and leadership and a pioneering spirit. He is the masculine principle of the builder, the doer and the visionary. In Greek mythology he is Zeus, a father or a patriarch. In Jungian psychology he represents the animus or the masculine principle. He is confident making life stable and secure for himself and others.

### V ~ The Hierophant

The Hierophant, sometimes named the High Priest, represents the archetypal principle of learning and teaching, knowledge to mankind. He has intelligent awareness and is committed in matters of the heart, mind and spirit.

### VI ~ The Lovers

The Lovers archetype symbolizes the art of loyalty and commitment in relationship, not only to a lover but also to friends, family members and colleagues. Such a person may make choices based on momentary gratification or based upon the greater good of all. Usually choices are made in the name of love are neither easy nor straightforward. They result in complications and repercussions.

## VII ~ The Chariot
The Chariot archetype represents the universal principle of change and movement, a combination of stillness and activity in undertakings. It is a vehicle for choosing changes for oneself. This archetype can point to a possible journey or mission.

## VIII ~ Justice
The Justice card symbolizes alignment and balance. This archetype analyzes and compares factual and false information in the process of truthful negotiation. It is the archetype of the mind that is balancing and synthesizing ideas often expressed through writing, research and design.

## IX ~ The Hermit
The universal principle of completion, contemplation, and introspection typifies the Hermit archetype. He is the wise person who draws upon his inner resources and experiences to assist others through life's processes. The Hermit explores the higher transpersonal realms of consciousness to discover inner truths.

## X The Wheel of Fortune
The archetypal Wheel of Fortune symbolizes perpetual motion, reflecting a continuously changing universe in the flow of human life. It is the dispenser of what is both positive and negative in life, moving towards progress and change.

## XI ~ Strength
This archetype represents the natural strength we contain in our nature to quell the instinctual beasts or personal demons within. It bespeaks of our inner coping resources and our capacity

to overcome temptation, manifesting itself as strength of character, courage, determination, accomplishment and physical strength.

### XII ~ The Hanged Man

The Hanged Man represents surrender and acceptance of the deeper aspects of who we are. He is in a position of suspension in which truth and realization are revealed, hanging between moments of decision. It is the archetype of considering alternative options and solutions.

### XIII ~ Death

The Death card symbolizes detachment and release. The archetype of the reaper sweeps away all the confining conditions so that rebirth and regeneration can begin. In most instances this card represents change, not the death of the body. However, it can refer to issues of death, fear of death, or death of someone from the past.

### XIV ~ Temperance

Temperance represents the archetypal principle of harmonizing opposites, balancing both the positive and negative elements of life. It is the archetype of right proportions, right timing and right intentions.

### XV ~ The Devil

The Devil represents our need to face our problems with mirth and humor. This symbol also represents the universal principle of sensuality and sexuality or the law or attraction and resonance. This devil is not evil but, in the Greek sense of the word, a genie or daimon. The daimon is a chaotic force of nature, the emissary in our soul's journey that seeks to shake things up to make us work at finding other ways of being conscious. Finally the devil may also symbolize the shadow side of our personality—those parts of our personality that we do not like to acknowledge.

## XVI ~ The Tower

The Tower is the archetype of change and awakening that is required to demolish the old, artificial and false parts of our natures. It also symbolizes healing, renovation, restoration and growth. It represents a choice to tear down what is no longer useful in our lives.

## XVII ~ The Star

The Star archetype represents the self-sufficient personality through which Spirit can actualize, brings innovative and creative ideas to life. It embraces the celestial mandate of looking within and trusting what is there so that we can manifest pioneering ideas and mystical visions.

## XVIII ~ The Moon

The Moon is the universal principle of making authentic choices to overcome illusion. This archetype also represents the feminine principle: quiet, contemplative and meditative. It brings awareness and harmony into the present.

## XIX ~ The Sun

This image symbolizes teamwork, partnership and collaboration. It is the creative life force within that is waiting to be used and expressed. It represents the masculine principle of cooperation and a shared creative vision embracing our ability to accept life as it comes.

## XX ~ Judgment

The Judgment card represents good judgment and discernment in personal, professional, and legal situations. It involves objective observations, direct communication and giving birth to new ideas in both family and career situations.

## XXI ~ The World

The World represents the universal principle of individuation and self-actualization. This archetype symbolizes the completion and integration of ones inner work, unifying polarities, oppositions, and paradoxes within oneself.

This is the self-actualizing person with fully expressed individuality with a capacity to be at home in the external world. It can also mean the positive end result of undertakings.

Chapter Six

# Using Tarot in Counseling

*I Am Teacher*

 

 

**T**AROT COUNSELING is a centuries-old art, yet it is a new tool to the health care profession. A well-trained practitioner can use Tarot to unlock hidden avenues of learning and healing in others. Helping them access inner wisdom in the healing of emotional and spiritual wounds.

As a transpersonal counselor, I understand how to achieve optimum states in the mind, the body and the spirit. This knowledge helps me guide my clients to their higher psychological and spiritual potential. Towards this end, I rely upon the archetypes to give me information.

After many years of experience with the cards, I know the archetypes because I have studied their expression through me. I realize that I cannot teach something I don't understand and haven't experienced. Therefore, during my assessment, I can tune into the archetypes being expressed through the client's body language, through their voice intonations, the way they dress and my intuitive impressions

## Client Assessment

During the initial assessment and client history I determine who will be a candidate for Tarot counseling. This decision is intuitively and intellectually based upon their physical appearance and my assessment of their ego strength, cognitive abilities and emotional state.

With a background in psychology and psychiatry I identify people who have a weak sense of the self or ego. The potential danger of any therapy that reaches beyond the ego is that of undoing the ego's defense mechanism and unleashing traumatic memories. This can cause a regression to a more primitive stage of development.

Part of my assessment is based upon my observations of the client's choice of clothes. In a nutshell, their prominent archetypal energy is dressing them. For instance, One day a new client, we'll call him Bill, came to my office dressed in jeans, white tee shirt with the sleeves rolled up over his biceps. A large animal tooth hung around his neck. On his head he wore a hat like the movie character Crocodile Dundee a rough and tumble masculine type. Since this man was over sixty, I saw this as an attempt to hold onto his fading feelings of youthful strength. I suspected that he was compensating for something. As it turned out he was sexually impotent.

When working with Tarot, the clients must be able to follow a train of thought and have the capacity for insight. The clients' ability for *symbolic thought* won't become apparent until counseling begins. This entails making associations between images on the cards and specific events in their lives.

It is easier to counsel people who are capable of this form of symbolic thinking, but not essential. When clients have difficulty thinking symbolically, I explain the metaphors and images at a level they can understand, and then ask them to apply it to their issues. For example, Dale, a 35 year old college professor, came to see me because he had poor self-esteem. I had Dale draw one card to aid our discussion. Dale drew the Page of Cups. The card shows a youth holding a cup with a fish inside. Even though the card represented him, he couldn't relate to any of the images. Because I knew him, I described his intelligence and his talents in detail. Then, I added, "The Page's energy is young and it isn't as mature at the king." I pulled the King of Cups from the deck and laid it on the table next to and in front of the Page card. In this card, the King of Cups calmly sets on a throne with a cup in one hand and scepter in the other. Water, which symbolizes emotion, swirls beneath his feet. I added, "The King of Cups has his emotions under control, he is mature, capable and confident."

Dale said, "Oh, now I get it. I am young like the page and not a fully developed like the king. I have a lot of life learning yet to do." He sat thoughtfully, for a moment then said "But I have been expecting a lot from myself." We then discussed the high expectations he had for himself. With these two Tarot cards, Dale came to understand the effect his expectations were having on his self-esteem.

Explaining the symbology of Tarot cards is also difficult with individuals who are concrete in their thinking. I call this the *materialistic personality*. They look outward at the real world while the inner world remains unrecognized. This type of person has no communication with their inner worlds. To these individuals, the cards look foreign, but it may be just the kind of *exploration therapy* a client needs. Their healing can be greatly aided by beginning a rapport between their conscious material worldview and their unconscious symbolic worldview.

An example of the materialistic personality is Alan, a furnace system's engineer. He asked the question of the Voyager Tarot deck, "How can I have more passion for what I do in my life?" He continued, "I can think of plenty to do but I can't get passionately involved in any project. Even my relationship lacks passion and real commitment."

The first three cards' that were laid out validated Alan's predicament. The fourth card, entitled "Regenerator" and "Sage of Cups," gave him his answer. This card shows: a native man who appears to be in a state of wonder as he lets water run through his fingers; Another man appears to be pouring water, from a vessel, over a fertile valley; in the corner of the card, two elderly people are shown laughing joyously. Alan said, "The images on this card are all happy. They seem to be finding pleasure and fulfillment in the things they are doing. This is what I want."

I asked him "When you feel happiness, where in your body do you feel it?" He thought for a moment then indicated the area of his heart.

"Whenever you are engaged in an activity take a moment to *check in* with this area of your body," I suggested. "If your heart is engaged in the activity, pursue that course. If you feel no passion, consider changing your course."

I paused to see if he understood then said, "Check in with your heart's intuition about everything. Using this kind of measurement is called *following your heart.*"

"The Sage of Cups is wise in the ways of the heart. This card is saying generate happiness through finding the things that give you pleasure. Learn to cultivate the joy of living." After a brief discussion about the logic of such an endeavor, he replied, "This is an interesting concept. I will try it."

Two months later, I received a postcard from Alan telling me about the positive affects the reading had on his decision-making. In his note, he mentioned that his participation in life's choices has more dimension. He had opened to his inner worldview.

### Giving Readings

Several minutes are spent in prayer and meditation before I see each client. I close my eyes, finding a place of centered calm, and wait. In this meditative state, I access the higher levels of my consciousness. Sometimes imagery or thoughts come, which give me information and inspiration. Sometimes it is a simply a restful silence before the session.

When I use Tarot cards, my assessment of the client's ego is important. The ego's purpose is to keep overpowering and destructive emotions within safe boundaries. It needs to be strong so it can integrate and use the emerging unconscious information. I distinguish between clients with *psychological limitations* and those individuals of a more normal constitution. Most clients that come to me have a normal constitution. They have a healthy ego structure, emotional flexibility, and a somewhat positive self-image. These clients benefit greatly from the *symbolic exploration* that Tarot provides.

An example of a weak ego is Sue, a client who requested a Tarot reading. During the session I could tell by her facial expressions that she was receiving profound information regarding her question. Instead of telling me about the insights she skirted the issue by talking about superficial aspects of the cards. She guarded her fragile ego by denying most of the surfacing messages.

In the therapeutic context, The Tarot spread allows the counselor to aid an individual in bringing repressed unconscious material to consciousness. The counselor should be able to evaluate when and how to aid the individual in this process. A reading could cause a release of emotions which are locked in the unconscious and which might overwhelm the weak ego with too much information, too fast. This could cause confusion and a scattering of the client's defenses.

After discussing *presenting issues* with the client and deciding that Tarot cards will be an effective tool, I have the client to choose between one of two decks: the Osho Zen and the Voyager Tarot. The Osho Zen deck has lovely and expressive artwork. The author's interpretations are based upon Buddhist philosophy. The Voyager deck uses familiar contemporary symbols grouped in photographic collage. I have clients look at both decks and choose the one they feel drawn to.

During the session, I shift my consciousness so that I am an empty vessel, freely associating to the information that comes to me. This shift allows a higher level of consciousness to work through me for the well-being of the client. I trust my intuition and higher psychic faculties. Because the information must come through my ego with its projections, I accept a margin of error. I never insist upon being right and frequently check my perceptions with the client to verify accuracy.

Some practitioners like to tape their therapeutic sessions. This is particularly valuable for clients who have difficulty listening or feel so stressed that their information intake is decreased. Taping a session is also an excellent way for clients to keep an accurate record of their *healing journey*. You can also ask your clients to write down their question. This helps them narrow their focus to a more specific idea within the issue, and you can encourage them to use the pad to take relevant notes.

After the question is written down, I ask the client to shuffle and cut the cards, poker fashion, in any way that is comfortable to them. I either lay the cards out on the table or hand them to the client one at a time and wait for a response. If they don't respond right away, I might ask, "What's happening in the card?" or "What symbol stands out for you?" In my experience, I have found that readings are more effective when client hold the card and examine it closely. I keep their question in mind, and refer back to it often during the session, saying, "How does that relate to your question?"

A Tarot reading takes about thirty minutes; however, I once had a four-card spread with a therapeutic discussion last several hours. The amount of time one takes depends upon the scope of the client's issues and the counselor's willingness to pursue it.

For the purposes of charting, I suggest having a ready-made form for note taking. List the deck used, the question asked and have room for relevant comments and objective impressions. It is easy to remember the crux of the reading but often one can't recall the question exactly as stated, so I write down the question verbatim and wait until the session is over to add the rest of the information. The counseling process should not be interrupted by note taking.

I propose that the body is a temple for the energy of the archetypes. In the chaos of the shuffle, the cards react to the energy of the shuffler's archetype of the moment. So much so that when the client's hands shuffle the cards, the energy of the heart Chakra with all it's archetypal energetic information affects the cards. The cards magically fall in line with a synchronicity that is part of the mystery of the cards. The resulting segmented pictorial layout is a portrait of the client's psychological state or their inner worldview.

Because the cards are shuffled with the hands and are most affected by the heart Chakra energy, emotional issues often take precedence over more cognitive or linear types of questions. For instance the cards may hint at current issues with an ex-husband even though the question asked was whether or not one should paint the house.

The archetypal images on the cards reflect a truth that is buried in the preconscious and unconscious mind. Through a process of projection, questioners come to see their issues, themselves, and others mirrored in the symbols of the cards.

Many times during the session I ask, "How does this image make you feel?" Because clients possess the archetypal energy symbolized in the card, they can connect at an emotional level using projection. I ask them to describe what they see and feel and how it all relates to the question.

Like the Rorschach Projective test, relating to the archetypal images on the cards brings forth seeds of information buried in the unconscious mind. I teach clients to understand the symbology of the card and relate it to their feelings and to their life situation. Only when this unconscious symbolic material becomes conscious can they take the appropriate action, which also may be mirrored in the cards.

When the initial session is complete, other issues may surface. I might choose to do a second reading, often I simply ask the client to pick several cards at random from the deck fanned across the table to address these secondary issues.

The counselor is not the authority over the client's situation. Rather, you should empower the client by letting his or her ideas lead you. Don't try to predict what will happen in the client's future. This would be fortune telling, filled with presumptions and inaccuracies. The counselor may, however, discuss possibilities and opportunities that may affect the future.

## Messages from the Archetypes

The counselor helps make the nature of the client's challenge clearer. The goal of the therapeutic session should be self-development and self-healing, and since there are always multiple levels of meaning in Tarot's archetypal images, the counselor can help the client to integrate those meanings which seem most useful.

The counselor should keep in mind that each card dealt is only an indication of what may be an issue for the client. Clients should be free to explore only those issues that they feel ready to deal with, at their own pace, for they are the only ones who can bring this awareness into *their* consciousness. The process is a gentle, sacred one and the cards should *never* be used to confront clients on issues they aren't ready to face.

Keep in mind that because a Tarot reading reflects the inner profile of the person shuffling the cards, only the client can say whether an interpretation feels right. For example: Roy had taken his new girlfriend on an expensive vacation. Upon his return he came to see me about the frustration and disappointment he felt because she did not have sex with him.

During the session, Roy's attention focused on the image of a firecracker on one of the cards. My impression was that the firecracker represented Roy's anger or sexual frustration in the situation, but I said nothing and waited for his response.

Roy eventually said, " I see the firecracker as representing a strong emotional charge. I see this as a spiritual challenge because I could easily resort to a *victim stance* and be angry. Instead, I want to look at the situation to see what my part in it has been." In this instance, my client's thinking was more sophisticated than my own initial projections.

Roy's case illustrates why counselors should be aware that their impression of the cards might be their own projections. Those projections are who *you*, the counselor are, and how *you* see the client in the moment. The projection may be an accurate impression, but if your interpretation is not true for the client, then it should be set aside.

I hold my interpretations back until the client has fully expressed the associations that he or she has for the imagery of the card. If I choose to offer my interpretation of the card, it is simply to add or expand upon the multiple dimensions of meaning. This can help a client make further associations to the issue at hand. Another example: Sarah had asked for a Tarot reading because she felt ongoing anxiety. The first card entitled "Control," depicted an uptight man with clenched fists surrounded by sharp geometric shapes. When Sarah saw the card she laughed. "That is me trying to control things."

I said nothing and *actively listened* for her insights. I then described some of the card's attributes. "This is the King of Swords," I said. "At the lower levels he needs to be in control. He thinks too much and doesn't value other people's viewpoints. Because he is good at thinking he believes he is always right."

Sarah replied, "This is true. Sometimes I talk so much I can't even hear what the other person is trying to say." With this comment I knew she was relating to the archetype and integrating the information.

Sarah's truth was accessed from the inside out. Further, she was able to take in my suggestion and integrate it along with her own truth. The insights were more powerful because she was able to make them hers.

### Counseling Card Layouts

Traditionally, there are numerous layouts available. For the purposes of transpersonal assessment and counseling I use a four or five-card layout or spread depicted in the Quantum Approach below.

I find this spread usually reveals one or two major focuses that will help the client in their growth. It helps them to clarify, understand and transform one or two thinking patterns, belief systems, or attitudes.

1. The first card represents the current problem. It is portrait of the question being asked. This card helps identify and clarify issues of the question.

MESSAGES FROM THE ARCHETYPES

## THE QUANTUM APPROACH

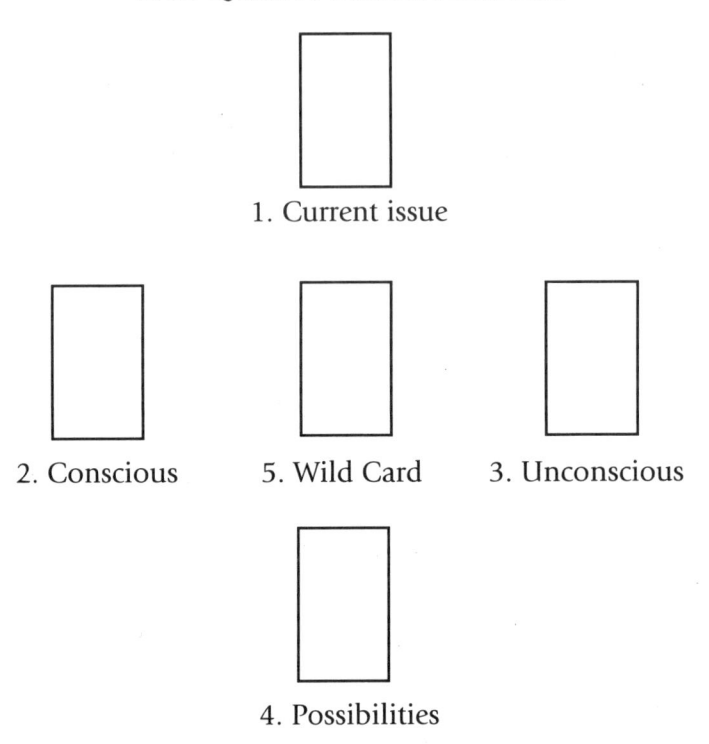

1. Current issue

2. Conscious   5. Wild Card   3. Unconscious

4. Possibilities

2. The second card reflects the conscious elements of the situation and usually represents something that the client is aware of.
3. The third card represents the preconscious and unconscious levels of the mind and represents issues that are below waking consciousness.
4. The fourth card is in a position closest to the client and represents possibilities. This card usually holds an answer to the client's question and can be seen as an outcome card.
5. The fifth card is the wild card and I use it to give additional information. It may not be necessary and I only use this card when more clarity is needed.

## THE LINEAR APPROACH

This technique can be used with virtually all clients. It is more concrete in its application and it appears that the choice of the cards has a cause and effect. Sometimes I use it during my assessment phase with a new client. Watching them choose gives me additional data about how they process information

An initial shuffle is not needed. Instead, the client holds the deck with the faces up and is instructed to look at the cards and make two piles: One pile of cards they like, and another of those cards they don't like. Ask them to do this quickly so it becomes more of an *intuitive choosing* than a thoughtful one. When they have completed the two piles, remove the pile they don't like.

Ask the client to repeat the process until they have four or five cards left. The counselor can then use the cards in the Quantum Approach layout.

Chapter Seven

# Tarot Case Stories

*I Am Healer*
*I Am Healed*

The following case stories demonstrate how the Tarot cards can help provide a therapist or counselor with a pictorial assessment of the client's state of mind. They illustrate the emotional investment a client holds and various ways to help him or her to access inner levels of consciousness for insights and solutions. During the counseling session I am deeply involved in the process of active listening, becoming receptive to intuitive impressions and honoring the sacred by focusing my awareness on the synchronistic collaboration between Spirit, self and other. I trust that the creative process will unfold for the benefit of the client.

Keep in mind that the name of the suits can change according to the artist-author of a particular Tarot deck. For instance, in some decks, the suit of Cups may be called Water, but it continues to represent the emotions. The suit of Wands may be called Fire, but it still represents the active sensations of will, passion, creativity and intuition. The suit of Swords may become Air, representing the mind or intellect. In the same vein, the suit of Pentacles may become Disks, Earth or even Rainbows, but it still represents the material world.

Moreover, the author of the deck may change the archetypal principles according to various themes. During the counseling session I either follow the author's meaning by reading it with the client or I can follow and work with the client's projection of the symbolic images. As with dream work, the meanings of the symbols on the cards can have a personal interpretation and I always consider the client's interpretation the right one.

### CASE # 1: Dealing with Stress and Anxiety

Phil, a 75-year-old retired orthopedist, came to me requesting advice on ways to reduce his stress and lower his blood pressure. After a thorough physical evaluation by his physician, he was placed on medication for hypertension. " I have periods where my heart races." He said, "When this happens I think that I am going to die."

After talking with Phil for a short time, I had the impression that he was denying, through intellectualizing, his fear of death. He knew the right terminology for his condition, and he over-analyzed everything. This kept his mind so busy that he didn't have time to acknowledge his feelings. I sensed he wasn't emotionally connecting his feelings to the idea that he was near the end of his life and the anxiety this would provoke.

Phil agreed to the use of Tarot cards and chose the Osho Zen deck. After some deliberation he asked, "What do I need to know to take care of myself?" I then directed him to shuffle the cards while thinking about the question.

The first card was entitled "Rebirth," number ten in the suit of Clouds (Swords). The traditional meaning of this card is the archetypal principle of endings and beginnings. The Osho card depicts a young boy, playing a flute as he emerges, like a spirit, out of the side of a lion. There is a camel in the lower part of the card with clouds or smoke around it. Because this card usually indicates a transition, I thought this could indicate that Phil had decided to face up to his feelings of anxiety and what they were trying to tell him. He, however, had other interpretations.

Since there were several images on the card, I asked Phil to describe those that drew his attention. "I am attracted to the young boy playing the flute because I like music," He said. He thought for a moment then added, "The camel, I think, represents my girlfriend's smoking. I ask her not to smoke around me because I know it is bad for me and I'm afraid of having a heart attack."

After a short pause I asked, "How do you feel about death?" He stated, in a matter-of-fact way, "I am not afraid to die."

I waited but he did not offer more for he either wasn't afraid of death or he wasn't ready to verbalize his feelings. I honored his feelings and drew the next card, "Suppression," number ten in the suit Fire (Wands). The traditional meaning of this card is the archetypal principle of excessive pressures. The Osho card shows a distressed man tied up in heavy ropes, with blood vessels pictured on the edge of the card.

Phil easily identified with the image, and said, "This is my physiology under stress." This opened a discussion about the ramifications of continued stress and how it could affect his health.

The third card was entitled "Going With the Flow," the Ace in the suit of Water (Cups). The card represents emotional perfection, and shows a human form relaxed and floating down a flowing river.

I asked him how this picture related to his question. There was silence as he looked at the card and when he didn't respond, I explained, "The suit of Water represents emotions and is the Ace is the ultimate positive emotional state. This card, in the Osho deck, represents a state of carefree relaxation and an acceptance of life."

"This is the state I want to get to," Phil responded. We talked about the differences between this state of relaxation and the stressed state he identified with in the "Suppression" card.

The fourth card in the reading was entitled "Postponement" number four in the suit of Clouds (Swords). This card is the archetypal principle of stillness at the point of completion and the image shows a gray person in a gray world looking through a window towards a color-filled landscape. Phil said, "This is me looking towards a brighter future."

This interpretation made sense to me and I asked him if he could *think* of anything else. He said no and I then asked him if he *felt* finished with this card. His eyes briefly looked down towards his solar plexus before he spoke. "It feels done," He finally said. For a brief moment, he had tapped into a non-threatening feeling state. It seemed to me that he had genuinely and deeply checked in with his feelings, but I still didn't feel that we had come to a conclusion.

I threw in a fifth wild card to encourage Phil to go further with the flow of his associations. If at any time during a reading, you feel that a deeper exploration is called for you can draw an extra card.

The next card drawn was called "Silence" number seventeen of the Major Arcana, traditionally entitled The Star. The traditional meaning of this card refers to the archetypal principle of going within and becoming one with your spiritual self. The image on the Osho card features a serene face with closed eyes superimposed on a starry night sky. This image led us into discussion about the benefits of mindfulness meditation. I hoped that meditation would help put him in touch with inner levels of consciousness to gain insights in order to relieve his anxiety. I didn't feel he could achieve this in talk therapy because, during this session, he remained analytical and intellectually preoccupied.

I had originally planned to teach him mindfulness meditation and as luck or synchronicity would have it, the cards validated my assessment and displayed a pictorial reference to reinforce my advice.

## Case # 2: A Warrior Personality

Trudy, a woman in her late forties, was diagnosed four years before with a large gastro-intestinal stromal sarcoma. She began seeing me soon after the cancer was detected. Trudy was a stubborn and determined person, a *warrior personality* and during her first session she exclaimed, "I am not going to die." Despite a pessimistic medical prognosis, difficult chemotherapy and three major surgeries, she is still thriving.

Trudy is at her best when she feels like she is in the driver's seat, and she feels under control when she can take part in her treatment planning. Because of her strong personality, one of her challenges has been to give up selfish ego level control and allow Spirit to work in her life. In part, she learned to give up hyper-analytical planning and be open to what we began to call "whatever needs to happen next." She learned how to keep her self-determination while finding a place in herself where she could set rigidity aside. This allowed for spontaneous creativity in her healing.

Over the years, Trudy and I have worked with many of the healing arts. We have used dream work to search the unconscious for healing clues; guided imagery to access an inner healer; meditation to calm the body and boost the immune system; energy work to replenish and clear her energy. This day, she came specifically for a Tarot reading. True to her independent personality, she said, " I don't have a question, I just want to scatter the cards on the table and pick them up from there." I thought this would be a way to see what was on her mind and how she was feeling. She chose the Osho Zen deck.

The first card was entitled "Aloneness," number IX of the Major Arcana. Traditionally this archetype is called the Hermit and represents introspection and a coming to terms with the inner life. The image on the Osho card is of a person searching in the dark with a lantern held high.

"This card represents where I am right now," Trudy said. "When I first started coming to you I felt a different kind of aloneness. Then I was scared, now I am not." She had developed the higher traits of the Hermit archetype and she felt at peace with herself.

The second card entitled "Letting Go" was number eight in the suit of Water (Cups). The traditional meaning of this archetypal principle is emotional inertia, with an image is of lotus leaves gently floating on a pond. One can see ripples in the water, were one drop has just fallen from a moisture ladened-leaf above the surface of the pond. Trudy thought for a moment then said, "I feel this image represents the energy of my healing journey. I have gained an ability to allow the healing process to unfold by just letting go, trusting the Universe and being open to whatever needs to happen." To me, this was the comment of a spiritual warrior. She had learned to give up selfish agendas and follow the spiritually creative path to healing.

The next card, entitled "Totality" number five of the suit of Fire (Wands), reflects the archetypal principle of anxiety or striving. The Osho card has an image of three women swinging end-to-end on a trapeze high in the air. They are strung together, with their hands holding each other's feet. They appear playful and free, yet alert and interdependent. "I feel that this represents how I have learned to acknowledge and use my mind, my body and my spirit during my healing journey," Trudy said. Her interpretation confirmed that she was operating in the upper levels of this archetype where struggles were met positively and creatively. She was following a higher path towards healing.

The last card entitled "Creativity," number III of the Major Arcana. In traditional decks this is the Empress and represents feminine principles like nurturing and receptivity. The Osho card depicts a woman with a halo of stars. She is reaching for the moon and is surrounded by all manner of swirls, triangles, and squiggles that look like she is energetically creating something. The deck's author meant this card to represent the experience of creativity as an entry into the mysterious realms of life. The author states, "Technique, expertise and knowledge are just tools; the key is to abandon oneself to the energy that fuels the birth of all things. This energy has no form or structure, yet all the forms and structures come out of it." Without the interpretation of the author, Trudy reported, "Because of my illness, I have learned to allow my creativity to flow naturally. The healing arts have taught me how

## MESSAGES FROM THE ARCHETYPES

to notice and allow my creative self to emerge."

Trudy sat quietly a moment and then said, " I feel the most important message from this reading is to honor myself and my own creativity. It reminds me of all the creative tools I have learned to use. It also reminds me to honor my intuitive self as I listen to my body intuitions and do whatever feels right. At the same time, I must honor the intellect because it helps me make choices and speak my truths."

I was a proud teacher. Trudy had learned her lessons well. I felt her interpretations were in harmony with who she was at this time in her healing.

### CASE #3: Patience and Acceptance

Mary, a 42-year-old client with a diagnosis of breast cancer, came to see me. She told me that her doctor had just informed her about a reoccurrence of the cancer that they thought was gone. This time it had metastasized to the brain and the prognosis was grim.

My first encounter with Mary was in a cancer support group, three years before. Since then, I had seen her on an individual basis for guided imagery and movement meditation sessions. She was a quiet person and even though we had known each other for several years she was and difficult to draw out in conversation.

When I explained the use of the cards, she felt comfortable with them and thought they could be useful. I felt she was comfortable at both a thinking and a feeling level and was open to an exploration of her issue through the archetypal imagery of Tarot. She chose the Osho Zen deck and asked the question, "What do I need to know?"

The first card entitled "Laziness," was number nine in the suit of Water (Cups) and reflected the archetypal principle of happiness. This card appeared in the layout upside down or "reversed." The Osho card depicted a man sitting in a lounge chair with a drink in his hand and sunglasses on his face. "This card is telling me to take the time to relax and nurture myself," Mary said. We discussed ways she currently nurtured herself and the things she could do in the future. Since the reversed card indicates a change from the upright meaning, I thought it might mean that she was unhappy and wanted nurturing. But she was telling me she needed to find ways to nurture herself. I decided to explore this with her.

In the past, I had met her husband several times. He seemed concerned and affectionate and I could see an emotional bond between them. I suspected she wanted lighten his burden by taking care of herself as much as she could. I asked her if she was letting him nurture her. "After it is all said and done," I added, "he might need to feel he contributed to your care,"

Mary said, "I have thought of that, and I understand, but I really want to take the burden off of him as much as possible. I am allowing him to take care of me as much as I am comfortable." After some discussion, I knew that letting him shoulder some of her care was not easy for her, but I accepted her stance and we drew the next card.

The next card was entitled "Postponement" number four in the suit of Clouds (Swords). Traditionally, it embraces the principle of stillness at the point of completion. Again we see the image is of a gray person in a gray world, looking out a window to a colorful landscape. "This picture reminds me of my to meditational walk," said Mary. "I need to find another place to hike because where I now walk is rather dark and colorless."

(Notice, Mary had a different personal meaning for this card than Phil did in the card story above.)

I waited, neither of us had any more to say so I drew the next card, entitled "Sorrow" number nine in the suit of Clouds (Swords). This card illustrates the archetypal principle of unhappiness, with an image of a man wrapped in a brown blanket in front of a gray background. With his hand to his face he appears to be crying. "I have a tendency towards negative thinking and depression," Mary said.

A brief discussion followed about the effects of prolonged depression. I brought out my pictures of the immune system and discussed in detail how important it was in fighting cancer and other diseases. I told her, " It is good to acknowledge negative thinking and allow sad feelings but for the sake of keeping the immune system functioning optimally you should not let yourself get stuck in these feelings for long periods of time." The discussion ended after identifying tools with which she could lift herself out of the dark moods.

The fourth card is called "Patience," number seven of the suit of Rainbows (Pentacles), and refers to the archetypal principle of successful waiting. The image is of a pregnant woman with a calm countenance holding her bulging belly. The individual phases of the moon are depicted arched across night sky above the woman. The card's author, Ma Deva Padma, states that the imagery reminds us that all we need to do is to be alert and patiently wait. Mary saw it differently, she said, "This is my need to nurture myself."

In the image, I saw a woman, pregnant with end stage cancer coping with impending death. Owning my projection, I said nothing and let her lead the discussion that centered on identifying the attributes of self-love. "In this culture self love is not encouraged" Mary said, "but if you don't love and nurture yourself you cannot truly love and nurture others."

I accepted Mary's personal interpretation of the image. Because the card might indicate that she was calmly waiting to die, I asked, "How are you doing with the possibility that you might die?" She simply said, "I'm doing fine." She sat quietly, maintaining a calm countenance like the woman on the card. She seemed at peace and I felt that she was truly waiting well. I didn't feel the need to go anywhere else and it felt right to both of us to choose another card.

The next one entitled "We Are the World," is number ten in the suit of Rainbows (Pentacles): the principle of abundance and prosperity. The image is of the earth suspended in a universe of stars with a circle of human figures dancing around the earth.

Mary thought for a moment then said, " To me, this is a spiritual message and represents our divine nature. When you contemplate this picture it is difficult to feel bad about yourself." Her comments led us into a discussion about living and dying. Finally she quietly stated, "I am okay with my dying; others feel worse about it than I do."

Lastly, she asked me to make a copy of the picture, with my scanner, so she could place it on her home alter. "It reminds me that everything is just as it should be."

The symbols on the cards were perfect for this introverted person, for they helped her to express her feelings more fully than she had done in previous sessions without the cards.

## Case # 4: Recovery and Integration

Connie, a 45-year-old woman had lost her husband of 20 years in a snowmobile accident. Understandably she was having difficulty with her grieving process. I felt she was lacking a spiritual philosophy.

" I don't relate to traditional religions." Connie began, "I am looking for a way to live my life more gracefully and cope with the loss of my husband," she told me at her first counseling session.

During the last few months she had read books, journaled nightly and kept a record of her dreams, all of which helped her develop an inner wisdom. She liked Tarot readings, because, in her words, " They lead me to seek my answers within."

This final session, Connie chose the Voyager deck and asked the question, "Who am I?"

The first card is entitled "Sage of Wands" and "Seer. " It is the Knight of Wands of the Minor Arcana. The traditional meaning of this card is the archetypal principle of vision and inspiration. In the Voyager deck the image depicts a man with a joyful expression. There is fire behind him, which appears to be burning into many other images. Among the images is an owl, the symbol of wisdom. The author of this deck, James Wanless, meant for this card to represent a burning through to the eternal truths and living in the light of the Spirit. He states, "Enlightened living comes from working with a "spiritual discipline" —any path or technique that helps you transcend the physical self and personal ego."

Interestingly, Connie intuited the universal principle of the card: "The symbols of this card represent my search for wisdom." The presence of this card confirmed that a wise archetypal energy was active in her.

The second card, entitled "Equilibrium," number two of the suit of Cups. It represents the archetypal principle of emotional harmony and depicts a swan on a still pond with flowers and a cactus on its back. Connie immediately said, "This card represents my stable emotions." I thought to myself, she is getting good at reading her cards. I made a mental note to speak to her, after this session, about finding her own deck of cards for continuing her inner work.

The next card, the "Sun" is number XIX of the Major Arcana, and stands for the archetypal principle of life giving energy to a partnership. This card has several images: the face of the Sun God, two people on the beach, blooming flowers and a fish swimming in water. "This is my need to get away to a sun-filled vacation spot and have some fun," Connie said. "I have a vacation planned now." I had a sense she was also thinking of romance but I said nothing because it wasn't important to this session. Connie also had nothing further to say so I drew the next card.

"Death" is number XIII of the Major Arcana and symbolizes the archetypal principle of change. The death card never means actual physical death unless, as in this case, there is an actual death issue. "I feel this card represents the transitions going on in my life," Connie said, "which includes issues of life and death."

I never end a reading with the death card because it can be spooky to some people, so I pulled a wild card. The card entitled " Synthesis," is numbered eight in the suit of Crystals (Swords) and reflects the archetypal principle of the analytical mind. The Voyager card's images depict a mix of natural crystals and man-made computer parts. Connie couldn't relate to the images of this card so I read the author's interpretation to her: "This card represents the full and integrated use of all your mental faculties to bring together all aspects of an issue and have a complete picture."

Upon hearing this, she was able to make a symbolic connection. Connie said, "Oh, this represents my acceptance of my husband's death and of my gaining a philosophy to create balance in my life."

After a short discussion, we were both comfortable that our sessions together were complete. She had found the path to inner wisdom, which was helping her integrate her life's changes.

At the beginning of our Tarot sessions together, she had drawn a card that depicted a child of about three-years-old starting down a path surrounded by beautiful rainbow colors. In my imagination, I saw an adult Connie continuing down that same path.

## CASE # 5: Family Patterns of Behavior

Susan, a 35 year-old artist and Tai Chi instructor, came for a one-time one-hour session at the Breitenbush retreat center. She was a housewife with small children. With a stern but sad affect she told me she was seeking answers to relationship issues. She was a heavy set but good-looking woman and exuded a mixed presence of stubbornness and intelligence. She began the session with statements like, "My husband and children are difficult to live with. They make me mad when they don't do what I want them too. I spend much of my time worrying about what they are doing." In addition to her statements, I had a felt sense in the area of my solar plexus. I could feel a lower level of the archetypal energies present in her.

Susan had a strong ego and I felt I could be direct with my impressions. I queried her about her parent's personalities. "I notice a certain forcefulness in you," I suggested. "You are very determined and know what you want and when and how you want it. Is there someone else in your family of origin that has these same traits?"

She paused, thought for a moment and told me that there was. Because she was a highly intelligent woman, she quickly made the correlation between her personality traits and her mother's. "I haven't thought about things this way before," she said. "I don't want to be like my mother. She isn't considerate of other people's feelings and ideas and she just does what she wants to do."

"Inherited behaviors are passed down through the generations," I replied. "It takes awareness of them to change them." She said that she wanted to change these behaviors but didn't know how. By the time we put the question to the cards, I was seeing a softer more positive side to her personality.

Using the Osho Zen deck, she asked, "What do I need to know to make a change?"

The "Queen of Wands" also entitled "Sharing" was the first card of the reading. A court card, its traditional meaning is the archetypal principle of self-knowledge and self-actualization. Since this card was reversed it confirmed what I already knew. This woman was operating in the lower levels of the archetype. I didn't mention the reversal or the lower level behaviors to her but I pointed her in a positive direction. I told her "This queen is intuitive, creative, talented has abundant gifts that she enjoys sharing." By reading the card in this way, I led her mind and her feelings to the upper and more positive levels of this archetype.

After some discussion she said, "The Queen of Wands that you described is what I want for myself."

I continued, "Because this card is in your layout, this archetype is already present. You just need to practice manifesting it." Susan's eyes met mine and she nodded in agreement.

The second card entitled "Inner Voice," number II of the Major Arcana, the High Priestess, illustrates the archetypal principle of the cultivation of the spiritual self, and its image depicts a serene meditating face in a nighttime sky. Together, we discussed ways in which Susan could cultivate her spirituality. "I feel like I would like to make a place in my home for an alter," she gently replied. "There I could calm and center myself and meditate upon ways to have a better relationship with my family.

" You might also have greater creativity in your artistic endeavors," I added. She agreed.

The next card, " Politics" was number seven in the suit of Clouds (Swords), reflecting the archetypal principle of hopelessness or futility. The image shows a sinister looking man with a pleasant mask held half in front of his face. There is a large coiled snake on the table in front of the man. Susan immediately said, "This is me having to put on a happy face for my family when I feel more like the mafia man behind the mask."

We again discussed recognizing negative patterns in the self as well as some ways to make a change. "You can't change others by trying to control them," I said, strongly suggesting that she explore other ways of getting results.

The last card, "Adventure" is a court card, the Page of Rainbows (Pentacles). Traditionally it captures the archetypal principle of the successful and dependable person. The image on the Osho card is of a small girl, a toddler, walking from darkness into a rainbow of light. We discussed cultivating spirituality, but this time we talked about going about it in a child-like way, cultivating an attitude of wonderment, adventure, play and an openness to encountering the sacred in everyday. I knew she understood as she said, "It is certain that if I cultivate my spirituality, my relationships with others will be different."

This was a very strong reading and because it was a one-time session, I could only hope that Susan went out the door with a different attitude than when she entered. Maybe I will see her again, and if I do, it will be interesting to know if she followed up on the messages from the archetypes.

## GUIDELINES AT A GLANCE
### Getting Started

1. Work with the cards at a personal level gaining knowledge and insights about your traits and behaviors as you see them mirrored in the cards.
2. Search for a mentor with your values and ideals.
3. Remember that the archetypal imagery of the cards represent the universal laws that we experience as thoughts, feelings and behaviors.
    a. Cups or Water represent feelings, heart or emotions.
    b. Wands or Fire represent will, activity and intuition.
    c. Swords or Clouds represent the mind or intellect.
    d. Pentacles or Earth represent the body or the material world.
4. Look for imagery on the cards that resonates with you.
5. Become familiar with the levels of each archetype by identifying them in your self.
6. Be able to visualize each image so you will be able to guide clients in this kind of exercise.

*The transpersonal counselor who aspires to use this sacred system of Tarot cards needs to:*

1. Have a working knowledge of humanistic and transpersonal psychologies.
2. Focus upon psychological potential and spiritual development of the client.
3. Provide information in a simple, direct, and understandable way.
4. Trust the client's interpretation of the cards.
5. Be aware that Tarot is a powerful tool and should not be practiced upon individuals with known mental illness unless the practitioner is qualified to work with such clients.
6. See that client's ego is strong enough to integrate and utilize the material coming forth from the layers of the preconscious and unconscious mind.
7. Know that clients must be able to concentrate, follow a train of thought and have the ability for insight.
8. Do not use Tarot with clients who may be conflicted about its use.

**A brief summary for reading Tarot:**
1. Go through the deck placing the cards in an upright position.
2. Give the client a pen and paper to write down the question and take relevant notes.
3. Ask the client to keep the question in mind as they shuffle the cards.
4. Decide which layout to use. Keep in mind the layout is affected by the heart Chakra energy and the question should have an emotional basis.
5. Remind clients to pay attention to their feelings as they look at the cards during the session.
6. Teach the client how to understand the images and make associations to the issue in question.
7. Help the client clarify issues and lead him or her towards self-development and healing.
8. *Never* use the cards to confront clients on issues they aren't ready to deal with.

Section Three

# Levels of the Archetypes

Chapter Eight

# Archetypal Levels in Tarot Counseling

*I Am Above*
*I Am Below*

THE FOLLOWING CASE study is based upon an actual session and my client's archetypal expressions. Although his name and identifying characteristics have been altered, the core truths of the Tarot reading are intact.

**The Case of Noah**
When Noah called to make an appointment my initial assessment began. He told me he had been sleeping on the living room couch for four months and had quit his nightly alcohol drinking two weeks ago. He said, "My wife is so negative about everything I just can't stand her."

Noah went on to tell me he was forty-six-years-old, had been married twenty-five years, had two children, and owned his own business. I suspected that Noah was fairly well developed despite his present difficulties.

With the information of the initial telephone conversation,

and the fact that he was asking for help, Noah lead me to believe he had a strong ego and might benefit from the kind of transpersonal counseling that I offer. I agreed to see him for Tarot counseling.

Development is archetypal. Around the world people have to satisfy the lower levels of basic physical needs, like hunger, safety and belonging before they are able to pay attention to upper spiritual levels. The upper levels of needs are based upon inner spirituality, such as love of self and others and living your own truth. Awareness of this inner spiritual world leads people to further their development towards their potential. This is what Abraham Maslow called self-actualization.

Although Noah's basic needs were satisfied, he was having trouble. (Trouble is a symptom of someone operating at the lower levels of his or her archetypes.)

Noah was a heavy-set well-groomed African American, with healthy skin and eyes. When he approached me, gently took my hand and looked me in the eye. His gaze was soft and my intuition told me that he was honest and direct.

Noah told me that his marriage was difficult. "We fight every time we try to talk. The kids hear us and yesterday my son began crying over it. That did it. I knew I wanted to change something, but I'm not sure what."

Noah had been in traditional counseling. The therapist had given him an antidepressant but after a year, nothing had changed and he stopped going.

I brought out my Tarot cards and my illustrations. Because I am not a traditional therapist and my concepts are new to most people, I explain them in simple detail before I begin the card session. I told Noah that I was oriented towards transpersonal approaches. This included spiritual perspectives that address issues, which transcended the material way of being in the world.

"I approach counseling sessions with the intention of helping you grow towards your full humanness and your rightful potential, but first you must take care of your physical, mental, emotional and social needs in the material world."

Once you have mastered the *material worldview,* you can begin to develop your *inner worldview,* which includes the intuitive and psychic levels of your being, or what I call the archetypal spiritual self.[1]

I went on, "When your needs aren't being met, the energy systems of your body—your feelings, moods, sexuality, etc will be disrupted much like a large rock disrupts a stream of water. This weakens the body and can lead to physical illness and psychological problems."

"Most people are satisfied with just the material attractions in the world. They are simply surviving but this is an incomplete way of living. You can be fairly comfortable and not go any further in your development but there is so much more that one can experience in life," I said.

Noah looked at me intently; I knew I had his full attention. I said, "People who live on the material level have two kids, a double car garage, a motor home and a dual income—they think they have it all. But inside they don't feel fulfilled. Something essential is missing and they may get ill. They may even grow old before their time and die."

Noah thought about what I said and replied, "I have all of the material things I need but I know there is more. I just don't know what that is."

I went on, "People need to develop a higher love of self. This is not a selfish or vain love but a true knowing of your rightful place in the world. Sometime in your development you come to realize that you are a divine being and you belong to a divine world and a divine universe. As you love yourself, you love others. You cannot express true love unless you have it for yourself. But you can't just step over some threshold and become a self-actualized person."

---

1. I use illustrations of Maslow's Hierarchy of Needs and the Chakra system to guide me in my assessment and counseling.

> **Characteristics of the Self-Actualizing Person**
> - Self-actualizing people are conscious of their inner worldview and become contributors to the greater good of humankind and the earth. They feel a kinship to others and selflessly give of themselves.
> - Self-actualizing people have a mission in life and see life as meaningful. They are creative, filled with self-esteem and live life fully.
> - They have difficulties but they enjoy life most of the time. This is because they live in the present and don't look to the future for a time when life will be better.
> - Self-actualizers feel that life is a highly interesting journey and they enjoy exploring.
> - Peak experiences lead self-actualizers to more awareness in their life. There is an openness to new explorations, which allows them access to spiritual experiences.

Loving yourself is at the foundation; it is the gate to the higher self. And loving yourself requires a lot of *inner work*."

I then explained to Noah, as I do with all my clients, "You must do this kind of work yourself. I can give you certain tools to accomplish this, like meditation, visualization and dream work and I can use guided imagery and Tarot counseling to help you develop abilities such as symbolic thinking."

I looked deeply into Noah's eyes and said, "You must go where you haven't gone before, on a journey through your own inner consciousness, the inner worldview, to gain your spiritual gifts of wisdom and insight."

Noah sat quietly, and finally said, "This is very interesting. This is what I want, not only for myself but for my family." I nodded and had him pick a Tarot deck.

Noah chose the Osho Zen deck and asked the question, "Where do I go from here to find my higher self?"

# Using Tarot for Healing and Spiritual Growth

The first card, entitled "The Creator" was a court card, the King of Fire. This king represents the archetypal principle of intuition in concert with creative action. On the card a bald, red robed man sits before an oval shaped object. There is a glowing yellow light emanating from his solar plexus.

I handed Noah the card and asked, "What do you see here?" He was at a loss as what to say, and since this was Noah's first experience with the cards I offered my interpretations first.

Slowly and concisely I began, "The King of Fire is a active and creative person. At the lower levels he is busy striving for material things and isn't aware of his spiritual self. He can be power driven, selfish, intolerant and impatient of limitation, easily irritated and terribly dogmatic with his ideas. He may get physical symptoms because of blocked or disrupted energy."

Noah stared at the card and said, "Oh, that's me. I feel irritated with people most of the time, especially family and employees. I also have trouble with diarrhea and have terrible cramps." He placed his hand over the area of his second Chakra, which governs the energy of the lower intestines.

I continued, "When you are dominated by the material worldview you aren't connecting to your spiritual needs. You basically function from what I call your *primitive personality.*"

Noah was listening calmly and intently. I slowly and concisely continued, "If you are operating in the lower levels of consciousness, your behaviors will be concrete and based upon selfish needs of the ego. Your whole life will be focused upon life on a materialistic level."

"This is true," Noah said. "I just want to get the job done my way and to heck with what my employees or anyone else may want."

I paused to listen to his comments, and I felt that his ego was strong enough to tolerate a little negative feedback. "At this level there is fear and the primitive mind uses a lot of energy to exert control over the environment. As a means to accomplish this control, a person may play it safe by embracing a lifestyle with little risk choosing values that have been tried and found to work for others."

"This is amazing," Noah said. "How do you know this about me? I try hard to live a lifestyle like I think I should, but I feel frustrated and confined. My wife doesn't think like me, and I don't have anyone to talk to."

We briefly discussed ways that he could appropriately satisfy his needs outside of the marriage, such as finding a group that focused on issues he wanted to talk about.

I told Noah, "My job is to help you become more conscious about your self. What you do with this new awareness is up to you. As I see it, your current dominant developmental level acts like an organizer of your behaviors, but it is like a box of limited information."

"I understand that." Noah said, "I'm operating on automatic pilot and not giving a lot of thought as to why."

Then he asked, "OK, how do I get in touch with my upper levels?"

I then made a suggestion, "Focus on the inner worldviews of your heart." I said placing my hand over my heart. I said, "This has to do with speaking your own truth, listening to your intuition and getting in touch with your spirituality. When people operate from their higher mind, or higher level of consciousness, they have what I call a more *refined personality*."

Noah was alert and ready to hear what I had to say. Since my goal was to guide him to the upper levels symbolized by this archetype, I described various attributes of the upper levels of the King of Fire." The person in this card is full of new ideas and has creative vision. Intuitive and able to make quick decisions, he is optimistic, conscientious, honest and loyal. Best of all, he is a devoted father."

Noah said, "I can be like that too."

I continued, "At the upper levels King of Fire *predominantly* chooses the higher path. He is mentally and emotionally stable and has high self-esteem. He loves himself and he loves others. There a strength of character about him because he has achieved mastery over his environment and displays his competence to the world through his work."

I told Noah, "Abraham Maslow called this upper level person a self-actualizing individual."

" Tell me more about the self-actualizing part of our being," Noah said. "I feel like I am finding out things about myself that I didn't know."

"We all have gifts and talents we can use in the world for work and for pleasure," I continued. "Becoming self-actualized means that you discover them and become all you are capable of becoming."

It was clear to me that Noah had a sincere desire to know and understand the upper levels and self-actualization. He was polite, interested and made appropriate comments. There was more I could tell him about this level but I wanted to work with that information as he grew in awareness. Also, I didn't want to overwhelm him with too much new information. I like to keep my communicating stream of information small and simple.

I finished by saying, "Self-actualizing people are spiritually in tune with something greater that themselves. Some call it God. I call it Spirit." I looked at him and waited for a response.

Noah said, "I am in an Alcoholics Anonymous group. We call this spiritual concept our Higher Power. That works for me."

I said, "To become all you are capable of becoming, you must build a relationship with your Higher Power during your inner work. I cannot tell you any more about this journey into yourself because everyone's experience is unique. Spend time in prayer—exploring life's deepest questions. And then sit quietly in meditation waiting for the answer." I added, "Be ready to receive answers synchronistically from the world around you because our answers come from many places: the mouths of babes, our friends, television, reading and so on."

Noah's affect had changed. He was calm and had a sharper

Noah's affect had changed. He was calm and had a sharper awareness. I knew he was truly listening.

I ended this card's message by saying, "To self-actualizing people, the lower level behaviors take on less importance. When they display the more primitive behavior, they don't judge themselves harshly and see the situation as having value as a life experience. Their aim is to strive towards higher goals, accepting their shadow side."

Noah nodded that he understood. I pulled the next card, which was entitled "New Vision" numbered XII of the Major Arcana. Traditionally this card is the Hanged Man and is the archetypal principle of awakening to patterns that limit and restrict our growth and development. The image on the Osho Zen card is of a beautiful male dancer exotically and beautifully tattooed. He is facing upward towards a starry sky and is moving among geometric shapes. The shapes represent the many dimensions of life available to us.

Noah immediately related to this card. Smiling he said, "The dark area at the bottom of the card is where I have been. What you are calling the lower levels of consciousness. The man on the card is me, with a new vision of what I want to be. I want to become a self-actualizing person and live my life on a higher path."

When you are helping a client find out who they are—you are introducing them to their archetypes but that person cannot be reduced into parts and held there. Our personalities are dynamic and subject to change. For instance, when Noah is telling me of a higher vision for himself, he is contemplating the higher levels of that archetype but until he gains a sharper awareness, he may go home and continue to operate in the lower levels. In his unawareness he may become a victim to the problems of communication in his marriage and respond by meeting her at the lower levels, becoming defensive, angry and argumentative.

I handed Noah the next card, entitled "Friendliness," number two in the suit of water. This card represents the archetypal principle of love and is illustrated by two trees, —one pink and one yellow, —standing together with their upper branches and leaves intertwined.

"This card shows how I would like to be with my wife, but she is a twig." Noah laughed, unconsciously blaming her for their problems.

His comment indicated the lower levels of this archetype where one often finds misunderstanding and fighting—the sign of a troubled relationship.

Noah continued, describing what the "Friendliness" card evoked. "She is the mother of my children and I want to have a healthy relationship with her." I told him about the upper levels of compassionate understanding but he couldn't identify with the concept saying sarcastically, "That would be nice." We discussed his marriage situation but didn't come up with any immediate conclusions or solutions. He wasn't ready to elevate their relationship to a higher level at this time.

The last card of the layout was entitled "Letting Go," number eight in the suit of water. This card represents the archetypal principle of emotional stillness and surrender to life and pictures lotus leaves on a pond. A drop of water had just fallen from a leaf into the pond below causing a ripple effect.

Noah identified with the ripple. He said, "This reminds me that however I respond, to my wife or my employees, there is an emotional ripple effect. I am reminded to be more aware of myself and my effect on others." He sat back looked at me thoughtfully.

I went on, "At difficult times in relationship, we have a choice in the moment. We can respond from the lower levels and have a negative effect on the other. Or we can respond from the higher respond we effect first our family, then our society and eventually the world."

As the session came to a close, I gave Noah the assignment of spending time in prayer and meditation. I also suggested he start a dream journal. He agreed to both, saying he was glad he came to counseling. Noah went away from our session with enough information to begin changing his worldview. He had the beginner's tools and the instruction to begin the inner journey towards inner peace and happiness.

Most of us become self-actualized by working our way up a hierarchy of needs, developing our selves by gaining self-knowledge and self-confidence. In this way we learn our life's lessons as we heal.

As we become more aware, we can choose which level to live our lives, moment to moment. When we come to know this, we can more easily maintain emotional equilibrium; make every action a higher action, every thought a higher thought and every intention a higher intention.

Chapter Nine

# Levels of the Major Arcana

*I Am Ego*

For easy reference and general identification I have separated multiple aspects of the archetypes—or who we are—into two categories: the upper refined personality and the lower primitive personality. The energies of the archetypes are available to us to use in a dynamic and complex way, for we have different archetypal levels of consciousness, values and behaviors to choose from moment to moment.

Whichever archetypal level or path we choose sets the stage for what we want to accomplish and positively or negatively affects the outcome of our endeavors.

**The Refined Personality**

When people operate in the upper levels of their mental, psychological and spiritual development, they display more refined behaviors. When we access this part of our psyche we operate at our higher level of consciousness, which is sometimes called the higher mind. Here, we become aware that we can control and express ourselves in any way we chose and because we are choosing to authentically to display who we are, we may seem eccentric to others.

The upper level personality predominantly chooses a path of "right action," a Buddhist term that refers to ones ability to compassionately interact with the world. Such people are mentally and emotionally stable and have a high self-esteem. They love themselves and they love others, often demonstrating unique talents and gifts. Usually, they are idealists who demonstrate high social values (which may not conform to society's values) and actively or passively resist an unjust authority, because they are in the process of helping their culture grow.

The more refined personality actualizes innate gifts and talents and strives to become all that he or she is capable of becoming. There is a desire to go beyond everyday experiences to explore the mysterious, the chaotic and the unexplained. Those who are living predominantly in the upper levels are highly intuitive and spiritually in tune with something greater than themselves. They have mystical inclinations and enjoy physical, mental and spiritual health.

**The Primitive Personality**

In this stage of development, the lower levels of the archetypes dominate us and we express a more primal personality. Survival, tribal belonging and social cooperation are the primary things a person strives for. When we are operating at this level we are focused upon coping with life by gratifying our physiological needs: eating, sleeping, working, meeting basic relationship needs and maintaining secure shelter for self and family.

We seek affection from relationships such as family and friends, and although we may be cooperative, we may also be competitive and conditional in our generosity. We can give love but expect something in return.

When this level is dominant we often aren't aware that we have an inner consciousness; thus we exhibit a more concrete and materialistic way of being in the world. We will also tend to display black and white thinking, dreading the unfamiliar and clinging to the familiar by seeking safety in an undisputed life routine.

# Using Tarot for Healing and Spiritual Growth

At this level the world is seen as cause and effect. It feels like an unsafe place because we have little control over it; thus we seek to organize ourselves around rules and ceremonies. This pragmatic mind-set has a belief system or a religion that gives organized answers to an organized universe.

At these lower levels, our traits include aggression, fear, cruelty, manipulation, lying, dependence, victimization, fanaticism towards a religious doctrine or a cause and a lack of empathy towards others. We may find ourselves ill, addicted or beset by social and psychological problems.

Clients experiencing emotional pain and problems in their life may be predominately operating through the primitive personality, or the lower levels of their archetypes, and the archetypes to receive counseling will turn up in the cards. I actively listen to the clients as they tell me of their experiences at the lower levels; they need to be heard and you need to know the situation. I then lead their perception to the upper levels by talking to the more refined part of themselves. For example, Nancy had difficulty with personal boundaries. She tended to feel everyone's emotional pain and this trait was having an effect on her health. She was operating in the lower levels of the Queen of Cups concerned more about others and neglecting herself. As her counselor, I would cue Nancy not to get over invested in problems she couldn't do anything about by gently reminding her, "That is their journey—not yours." Nancy created an affirmation to help her stay focused on the higher aspects of life: "I am compassionate and have a Zen-like acceptance of things I cannot change." In this way, Nancy could begin to integrate the upper levels of the Queen of Cups.

## Levels of the Major Arcana

The twenty-two Major Arcana of Tarot have been given distinctive Roman numerals that count from I to XXI plus an unnumbered card known as the Fool.

The symbolic images on the cards represent major universal

principles or archetypes that operate in and through us. We experience these principles as the upper more refined and lower more primitive character patterns in our personality. These archetypes are timeless in that they have been with humankind since our earliest beginning and will continue as long as humanity exists.

The Roman numeral assigned to each Major Arcana card makes the Tarot easier to learn because it begins with the classic fools journey—a familiar theme in many myths, legends and fairy tales.

Like the hero's journey I outlined in Chapter Three it can be seen as a progression of psychological development we all must go through to achieve the upper levels and become a self-actualizating and more refined personality. Each numeral illuminates a stage of psychological growth leading to maturity and personal integration.

### The Fool's Journey

This myth begins with the birth of a hero (the Fool), which leads to the discovery of his personal power (the Magician). Coming to terms with his inner parents (the Empress and Emperor), he discovers his divine inner nature and reassesses his inherited values (represented by the High Priestess and the Hierophant). He has conflicts and choices to make in the arena of love (The Lovers) as he begins his worldly endeavors in adulthood (the Chariot). After many trials he acquires the fair witnessing mind (Justice) and emotional maturation (Temperance) as he learns to overcome nature's temptations (Strength). He spends time getting to know his inner life (the Hermit). Eventually, the Fool experiences some form of loss or crisis (the Wheel of Fortune). This evokes in him a need to change (the Hanged Man), which brings him to the gates of transformation (Death) this is followed by a journey into the underworld in order to discover what is responsible for this crisis (the Devil). He then makes changes in his outer life (the Tower). After his struggles with the dark forces, encounters the archetypal principles of the celestial bodies: (the Star) the ego's will recedes and a higher consciousness emerges (the Moon) feminine principle of receptivity and nurturing that begins with care of the self. The masculine principle (the Sun) successfully cooperates with others to make a difference in the world. This victory over the darkness results in rebirth (Judgment) and self- actualization—the complete person (The World).

## THE MAJOR ARCANA

### 0 ~ The Fool

The Fool represents a relative state of non-being, no fear, a going with the flow. This archetype is also the initial impulse to begin a flow of creativity in new endeavors. It is the stillness before action—the pivotal moment.

Upper Levels: Ecstatic joy. Anticipation and a sense of adventure. New feelings and new ways of being. Beginning of a heroic journey. Calculated risk. Initiative. Peak experience. Psychologically healthy and without fear. Open to the mystical, transcendent and transpersonal realms of consciousness.

Lower levels: Lack of discipline. Sexual impulsiveness. Impulsive acts in general. Irresponsibility. Immaturity. Irrationality. Insecurity. Unrestrained excess. Craze. Unbridled passion. Carelessness. Obsession. Mania. Inattention to important details. Indiscretion. Infatuation. Reluctance to listen to advise from others.

### I ~ The Magician

The Magician represents communication and directed will. He is clear in his intention towards others. He is able to manipulate people and situations. This archetype is in touch with his innate gifts and talents. He may use them for good or selfish purposes. One may see this will as coming from the invisible realms of our consciousness to manifest synchronistically in the world.

Upper Levels: Someone who is aligned with the will of Spirit. A higher will is directed through the ego and manifests as wise counseling and wise conduct. Inspired communication and vision. Communicating genius within. Ability to articulate thoughts and ideas clearly and succinctly. Right speech. Right action. Originality. Creativity. Ability to utilize one's capabilities in order to accomplish a task. Willpower. Imagination. Mastery and skill. Spontaneity. Self-confidence and self-reliance. Influential. Unity of thought and emotion. Ability to see task through to completion.

Lower Levels: Blunt. Ill timed or confused communication. Guile. Crafty. Deceptive. Slight of hand. Weakness of will. Indecision. Ineptitude. Insecurity. Lack of imagination. Manipulation. The use of one's innate gifts, talents and willpower for destructive ends.

### II ~ The High Priestess

The High Priestess is an androgynous archetype that represents the universal principle of inner resourcefulness. She has yin (soft and receptive) and yang (strong, dynamic assertive) energies. The balance of these energies are what determines the level that the archetype is operating.

Upper Levels: The inner journey or the return to one's self. Independence. Self-trust. Self-resourcefulness. Higher knowledge. Wisdom. Intelligence of a superior order. Spiritual insight. Sound judgment. Common sense. Higher education. Ability to teach others. Enlightenment. Intuition. Harmony and individuation. Ability to sublimate sex drives into a tool for self-development and self-actualization.

Lower Levels: Ignorance. Shortsightedness. Lack of understanding. Selfishness. Acceptance of superficial knowledge. Platonic relationships because of fear of intimacy. A tendency to avoid emotional entanglements. Shallowness. Improper judgments. Conceit.

## III ~ The Empress

The Empress represents humankind's ability to extend love and to receive love; the ability to extend one's self for the purpose of nurturing one's own or another's growth. The symbol of feminine productivity in action is often represented as Venus Goddess of love. In Jungian psychology she represents the anima or the feminine principle.

Upper Levels: The "good mother." Approaches life with an attitude of love and wisdom. Trusting. Balanced heart that gives and receives love in equal proportions. Gives mentally, emotionally, physically, and spiritually as appropriate. Healing power of love. Nurturing. Supportive. Unity of mind and heart. Ability to explore internal and external worlds with equal agility and personal confidence.

Lower Level: The "bad mother." Tendency to over give. Female guiles. Nagging. Vacillation. Anxiety. Infertility. Infidelity. Inaction. Dependency and lack of confidence.

## IV ~ The Emperor

The Emperor archetype represents power and leadership and pioneering spirit. He is the masculine principle of the builder, the doer and the visionary. In Greek mythology he is Zeus, the father or the patriarch. In Jungian psychology he represents the animus or the masculine principle.

Upper Levels: The "good father." Makes things stable, solid, and secure for himself and others. Adventure. Exploration. Royalty and leadership. Unity of mind, heart and spirit. Making decisions. Taking action. Nurturing. Accomplishment. Male influence. Firmness. Capable. Willing to listen but follows his own convictions. Confidence.

Lower Levels: The "bad father." Immaturity. Ineffectiveness. Lack of strength. Indecision. Weak character. Failure to control emotions. Works toward materialistic gain with little regard for his responsibilities of the heart. Lack of commitment.

## V ~ The Hierophant

The Hierophant, sometimes named the High Priest, represents the archetypal principle of learning and teaching. The teaching is the communication of specialized knowledge to humankind.

Upper Levels: Communication of the laws of the Universe in matter and in spirit. Goodness. Wisdom. Teaching in the name of truth. Capable of a higher understanding. Intelligent awareness. Commitment of the mind, heart, and action that are consistent and integrated. A vehicle for the realization of forms inspired by Spirit and is directed by Spirit. A capacity to walk the mystical path with practical feet.

Lower Levels: Lack of conviction. Timidity. Tendency to cling to dogmatic ideas. Over-kindness. Foolish exercise of generosity. Impotence. Vulnerability. Unorthodoxy. Renunciation. Fanaticism.

## VI ~ The Lovers

The Lovers archetype represents the art of loyalty and commitment in relationship, not only to a lover but also to friends, family members, and colleagues.

Upper Levels: Love. Truthfulness. Honor. Harmony. Intimacy. A gift of spaciousness such as allowing loved ones space and freedom to be themselves and not be barred, limited, and restricted in their other relationships. The beginning infatuation and possible romance. Child-like innocence, curiosity and playfulness. Passion. Compassion. Following what has heart and meaning. Clear on loyalties and priorities. Spiritual connection. Sincerity in making choices based on higher principles.

Lower Levels: Passionate illicit love. Reason obscured by feelings of love. Making choices based upon momentary gratification. Clinginess. Unreliability. Separation. Frustration in love and marriage. Fickleness. Untrustworthiness. Struggle between sacred and profane love. Yearning. Temptation.

## VII ~ The Chariot

The Chariot archetype represents the universal principle of change and movement, a combination of stillness and activity in undertakings.

Upper Levels: Choosing fortunate and abundant changes for one's self. Career changes. Riding the crest of success. Thoughts of a possible voyage or journey. A higher mission. Success when physical and mental powers are maintained in balance. Personal power effectively put to work.

Lower Levels: Unsuccessful. Defeat. Trouble and adversity in undertakings. Overwhelmed. Disturbed. Distressed. Failure to face reality. Vengeance. Fleeing from reality. Perplexity.

## VIII ~ Justice

The Justice symbol represents the universal principle of alignment and balance. This archetype reflects the analyzing and comparing factual versus false information and the action of truthful negotiation.

Upper Levels: Justice. Lifting the veils of illusion, delusion and deception. Truthfulness. Fair judgment. Authenticity. Legal or financial balancing. The mind that is balancing and synthesizing ideas. Ideas expressed through writing, research and design. The application of creative ideas in a positive way.

Lower Levels: Over analyzing. Doubting one's self. Confusion. False accusations. Bigotry. Severity in judgment. Intolerance. Unfairness. Unbalanced thinking and lack of insight.

### IX ~ The Hermit

The universal principle of completion, contemplation, and introspection typifies the Hermit archetype. He is the wise person who draws upon his inner resources and life's experiences to assist others through life's processes.

Upper Levels: Solitude. Introspection. Contemplation. Meditation. Attention to inner details. Exploration of the inner transpersonal realms of consciousness. Material expressions of deep inner truths, ethics, and values.

Lower Levels: Imprudence. Rashness. Immaturity in thinking. Foolish acts. Trouble with extreme introversion. Depression. Social ineptitude. Withdrawal from participation in life. Self denial. Overly self-conscious. Regression.

### X ~ The Wheel of Fortune

The archetypal Wheel of Fortune is the universal principle of the perpetual motion, of a continuously changing universe and the flowing of human life. It is the dispenser of what is both positive and negative in life.

Upper Levels: Special gain due to luck or individual effort. Godsend. Culmination. Conclusion or result. Positive influences affecting the outcome of a problem. Suggests the course of things from beginning to end. Prosperity. Opportunity. Abundance. A breakthrough inspiration.

Lower Levels: Negative influences affecting the outcome of a problem. Bad luck. Closed to taking a risk. Fixed opinions. Routine habits. Lack.

## XI ~ Strength

The Strength card represents the natural strength we contain in our nature to quell the instinctual beasts or personal demons within. This universal principle bespeaks of the inner coping resources inherent in our nature.

Upper Levels: Strength of character. Physical strength. Mental and emotional strength. Courage. Fortitude. Conviction. Determination. Resolution. Defiance. Confidence. Mind over matter. Accomplishment. Heroism. Virility. Strength to endure in spite of obstacles. Tireless efforts. Triumph of love over hate. Overcoming temptation.

Lower Levels: Weakness. Pettiness. Impotency. Illness. Tyranny. Lack of faith. Abuse of power. Succumbing to temptation. Indifference.

## XII ~ The Hanged Man

The Hanged Man archetype represents the universal principle of surrender and acceptance of the deeper aspects of who we are. The Hanged Man is in a moment of decision at which truth and realization are revealed.

Upper Levels: Recognizing repetitive patterns that bind, limit and restrict our growth and evolution. Pattern breaking. State of acceptance. Acknowledgement of "hang-ups." Considering options, solutions and perspectives other than the current ones. Sacrifice of the ego to pursue an inner worldview.

Lower Levels: Numb. Asleep. Depressed. Blind. Limited. Self imposed limitations. Repetitive destructive patterns in the personality. Life in suspension. Apathy. Boredom. Abandonment. Lack of progress. A pause in one's life. Lack of sacrifice. Useless sacrifice. Preoccupation with the material worldview. The sacrificial lamb.

## XIII ~ Death

Death symbolically represents the universal principle of detachment and release. The archetype of the reaper sweeps away the weeds symbolic of the confining conditions surrounding him so that the rebirth and regeneration can begin. In most instances this card does not represent the actual death of the body.

Upper Levels: Change. Transformation. Clearing the way for new efforts. The ending of a familiar situation or friendship. Beginning of something new. New ideas or development. Death. Rebirth.

Lower Levels: Slow changes. Immobility. Stagnant. Partial change. Inertia. Illness and fear of death or change.

## XIV ~ Temperance

Temperance represents the universal principle of harmonizing opposites. By finding a ground which transcends and encompasses both the positive and negative we come to know the archetype of balanced emotions.

Upper Levels: Balancing the apparent paradoxes. Oppositions. Polarities within our nature. Synergy or the union of two or more principles, which combined can create a greater whole. The balance and tempered being. Emotional equilibrium. Moderation. Patience. That which can be accomplished through self control. Emotional frugality. Harmony. Management. Compatibility. Ability to recognize and utilize the material and intellectual manifestations available to oneself. Exuding confidence.

Lower Levels: Emotional pain. Imbalance and extreme emotional states. Discord. Hostility. Inability to work with others. Difficulty in understanding others. Impatience. Frustrations. Too temperate to achieve a goal requiring assertiveness.

## XV ~ The Devil

The Devil archetype represents the universal principle of sensuality and sexuality or the law of attraction and resonance. This devil is not evil, rather, he can be seen, in the Greek sense of the word as a genie or daimon. The daimon is a chaotic force of nature, the emissary in our soul's journey. It seeks to shake things up to help us increase our consciousness.

Upper Levels: Facing difficulty with tenacity. Seeing the humor in problems. Release from bondage. Overcoming fear. Sacred sexuality. Androgyny. Natural force of attraction. Passion and power rising from the unconscious. Levity. Creative energy that wants to be expressed with mirth and party-making. Attraction to something or someone who motivates and evokes creative energies.

Lower Levels: Sexual problems. Deprived sexuality. Forbidden love and attraction. Subordination. Ravage. Bondage. Bad outside influence. Personality disorders. Temptation to do evil. Ill-tempered. Unethical principles. Inability to realize one's goals. Dependence upon another person, which leads to unhappiness. Negative moods.

## XVI ~ The Tower

The Tower is the archetype of change and awakening which helps to tear down that which is artificial, false or conditioned. Only then are old forms in our natures restructured. It is the symbol of healing, renovation, restoration and growth.

Upper Levels: Tearing down destructive personality patterns or worn out cultural norms. Choosing to dismantle that which no longer useful in your life. Healing aspects of oneself and one's life. Change in a complete and sudden manner. Breaking down of old beliefs.

Abandonment of past relationships. Breakthrough into new areas.

Lower Levels: Continued oppression. Following old ways that don't work. Living in a rut. Inability to affect a worthwhile change. Entrapped in an unhappy situation. Disruption and adversity. Misery. Loss of stability.

## XVII ~ The Star

The Star archetype represents the self-sufficient personality through which Spirit can actualize innovative and creative ideas on earth. The Star symbolizes inspirational ideas that serve others.

Upper Levels: Confidence and high self-esteem. Pioneering ideas. Self-love. Self-trust. Self-respect. Quality of looking within and trusting what is there. Becoming more spontaneous and flowing emotionally. Hope. Faith. Spiritual love. Fulfillment. Satisfaction. Pleasure. The proper balancing of desire and work, hope and effort, love and expression.

Lower Levels: Unfulfilled hopes. Disappointment. Pessimism and bad luck. Stubbornness. Bullheadedness. Imbalance. Low self-esteem. Inability to trust in the spiritual aspects of the self.

## XVIII ~ The Moon

The Moon is the universal principle of making choices based upon an authenticity that overcomes illusion. This archetype also represents the feminine principle of reflecting a light onto the world.

Upper Levels: Quiet and deep contemplation. Meditation. Awareness. Harmony with the Now. Authentic emotions. Overcoming illusion. Romantic inclinations.

Lower Levels: Delusion. Overcoming temptations. Illusion. Dishonesty. Ulterior motives. Insincerity. Selfishness. Insincere relationship.

## XVIIII ~ The Sun

The Sun archetype represents teamwork, partnership and collaboration. It is the creative life force within us waiting to be used and expressed. It symbolizes the masculine principle of assertiveness and cooperation.

Upper Levels: Cooperation. Teamwork. Shared creative vision. Creative process that involves the implementation of both our dynamic and magnetic expressions. Accomplishment. Contentment. Love. Joy. Devotion. A happy union. Pleasure in daily existence. A good friend. High spirits. Contentment derived from extending oneself to another human being. Ability to accept life as it comes and live contentedly.

Lower Levels: Unhappiness. Loneliness. Cancelled plans. Lack of friendship. Broken engagement or divorce. Triumph delayed and not necessarily lost.

## XX ~ Judgment

The Judgment card represents good judgment and discernment. This archetype is utilized in personal, professional, and legal situations.

Upper Levels: Consideration of the whole picture of a situation. Creative and professional power. Giving birth to new forms in both family and career situations. Forgiving ourselves and others. Inspired vision. Objective observation. Communicating judgments. Rebirth.

Lower Levels: Conduct towards other people is unfair and unkind. Taking unfair advantage. Failure to face facts. Indecision. Decision to divorce. Alienation of affection.

## XXI ~ The World

The World card represents the universal principle of individuation and self-actualization. This archetype represents the completion and integration of great inner work that has involved unifying paradoxes within oneself.

Upper Levels: The self-actualizing person. Fully expressed individuality. Capacity to be at home in the external world and at home within ourselves. Natural visionary. Highly creative. Innovative and original. Attainment. Perfection. Completion. Success. Capability. Triumph in undertakings.

Lower Levels: Imperfection. Fragmented. Developmentally delayed. Failure. Inability to complete a task. Disappointment. Lack of vision. Not being true to oneself.

---

**EXERCISE:** Working only with the Major Arcana, do a series of readings for yourself. As you become familiar with the meanings I have given in this chapter, allow your intuition to create personal meanings as well.

**Sample questions to try:**
What archetype expresses my higher self?
What aspect of myself do I need to develop?
Where am I in my development?
What do I need to know about [work, spouse, friend, situation]?

Chapter Ten

# Levels of the Court Cards

*I Am She*
*I Am He*

**I**n readings, the Court cards—the kings, queens, knights and pages—act as a human representative between the narrow activities of the Minor Arcana and the broad philosophical concepts of the Major Arcana. The Major Arcana represents the questioner's psychological state. The Court cards of the Minor Arcana expand the reader's information with details of relationships, personality traits and creative potentials in a more specific way. Some Tarot readers choose only to work with the Major Arcana—others prefer the subtleties and detail of working with the full deck.

The court cards act as a bridge between the Minor and Major Arcanas and can symbolize a numerous things: at the refined upper levels they represent sixteen types of self-mastery; at the primitive lower levels they symbolize sixteen types of traits used to cope with an angry and fearful world. They can represent the major personal archetype for the questioner or a significant other. For instance, In readings, my husband Lewis identifies himself as the King of Coins. The king, like Lewis, is adept at making things work in the material world. I see my son Ryan as being represented by the King of Wands. Like the king, Ryan is active, with a creative mind and a desire to display leadership qualities. I identify with the Queen of Swords as I use my intellect to organize and write this book but as a mother, I am represented by the Queen of Cups archetype, who acts with heart and good intentions.

The root of the Minor Arcana's symbolism may come from various quarters. One theory states that the Tarot emblems of the Court cards—the Wand, the Cup, the Sword and the Pentacle—were connected with the four Grail Hallows, or sacred objects found in the Grail castle of Arthurian legend. It was thought that these cards contained the secrets of the fourteenth-century Knights Templar, who may have had access to the inner mystery of the Grail.

## Archetypal Energies Represented in the Suits

Wands, or Fire represent the energy spark of divine creativity, which in psychological terms may be called intellectual intuition. It is the feeling of inspiration and inner certainty that forms an important beginning for the whole creative process. Wands can also represent new growth and an action in the world. Fire is active, male, life-giving energy.

Cups, or Water, symbolize the feelings and emotions which give depth to the creative urge represented by fire. The suit of Cups deals with inner experiences and emotional intuition. The water element represents heart energy and deals mainly with emotional relationships, happy or otherwise. Water is passive, feminine and nurturing.

Swords, or Air, represent the masculine intellect seeking out the truth and logic of life. Thinking is essential to sorting out confused ideas and emotions. The sharp intellect can be seen as the sword of truth.

Pentacles, or Earth, is a symbol for the material world of our physical being and needs. The earth provides the firm base from which we can explore and grow. The material level provides an essential basis for the creative intuitive, emotional or intellectual ideas to bear fruit. The symbol of the five pointed star, engraved on each pentacle, is a multidimensional glyph, representing the divine earthy vessel of the energetic divinity of our bodies. It also symbolizes the multidimensional nature of the world.

## Levels of the Court Cards
### Kings

The Kings stand for personal power and superior abilities and can represent males or females. They organize and make things safe but they need the help of the Queens to carry out their enterprises. At the upper levels they stand for authority and mastery.

### King of Swords

Upper Levels: Judgment. Intellectual prowess. The focused, intentional and determined mind. Receptive and dynamic thinking. Organizing. Analytical. Strategic skills of the mind. Scientific. Mathematical. Love of intellectual concepts of truth and justice. Authoritative. Commanding. A person of many ideas. A trusted advisor.

Lower Levels: Lacking in a depth of feeling. Non-emotional. Aloof. Unresponsive. Lack of compassion. Intellectualizes as a defense. Shallow. Untrustworthy. Intellectually dim. Judges harshly. Suspicious. Over-cautious.

### King of Wands

Upper Level: Leadership. Steady powers of concentration and will to manifest his vision. Master of wit and charm. Warm and generous. Good sense of humor and likes fun. Full of new ideas and has an abundance of vision and foresight. Intuitive. Able to make instant decisions. Optimistic. Conscientious. Honest. Loyal. Devoted. Fatherly.

Lower Levels: Power driven. Selfish. Intolerant of limitation. Impatient. Sore loser. Unorganized. Easily distracted. Easily irritated. Excessive ideas. Exaggerated ideas. Dogmatic. Irresponsible. Power hungry fierce competitor. Obsessive.

### King of Cups

Upper Levels: Artistic. In touch with the world of feeling with which he seeks to form relationships. Responsible. Creative. Kindly. Reliable. Considerate. Interested in the arts and sciences. Levelheaded. Dignity. A learned person. Wounded healer. Compassionate, empathic, counselor. Loving and fatherly.

Lower Levels: Artistically expresses pain and ugliness. Bad temperament. Double-dealing. Dishonesty. A person without virtue. Vanity. Arrogance. Seeks relationships that feed his or her ego. Superficial relationships. Moody and overly sensitive. Avoids growing up emotionally. Depression.

### King of Pentacles

Upper Levels: Ambitious. A person of character and intelligence. Affinity to manifest desires at a material level. Business acumen. Generous with possessions. Enjoys material possessions. Experienced and successful leader. Loyal friend. Reliable in marriage. Wise investments.

Lower Levels: Greed. Using any means to achieve the desired end. Unfaithfulness. Thriftless. Hedonistic. Desire for power and recognition in the eyes of others. Unconscious of his potential for corruption. Compulsive. Wants ownership of others.

## Queens

The Queens represent actual people, usually women, or parts of the client's personality. Like the Kings they stand for authority or mastery of the traits and behaviors of that suit.

### Queen of Swords

Upper Levels: Feminine intelligence. Logical. Analytical. Organized. Quick-witted. Intensely perceptive. Integrity. Loyal. Stable. Reflective. Strong willed and determined. Able to bear suffering with strength. Pride. Mathematical. Scientific. What the kings decide and mandate, the queens nurture and cultivate through the growth stages.

Lower Levels: Loneliness. Sadness. Narrow minded. Maliciousness. Bigotry. Deceitfulness. Vengefulness. Prudishness. Ill temperament. Unrealistic ideals. Aloofness. Perfectionism. Primarily identified with the masculine world of mind. Emotional frustration. Unforgiving. Judgmental.

### Queen of Wands

Upper Levels: Feminine charm and grace. Sharing. Intuitive and creative. Can sustain a vision until completion. Understanding. Friendly. Loving. Honorable. Practical. Capable of love and compassion. Sincere interest in others. Strong willed. Can run a home and family and still find time to vigorously pursue her own interests. Tireless versatility. Can have several projects going at once. Gracious hostess. Strong leadership and inspirational skills.

Lower Levels: Unorganized. Lazy. Jealousy. Deceit. Possible infidelity. Unstable emotions. Fickleness. Resistance. Obstacles. Opposition. Temperamental and stubbornly willful. Obsessions. Bossy and demanding.

### Queen of Cups

Upper Levels: In touch with the depths of her inner world of feeling. Capable of putting into practice her dreams and visions. Imaginative. Hypnotic power of the feminine. A deep emotional life. Warm-hearted. Loving intelligence. Practical. Honest. Beloved. Poetic. Artistic. Romantic ideals of relationship. Adoring friend and mother. Sexual relationships must blend love and ecstasy of spirit.

Lower Levels: Seductress. Uncontrolled passions. Inconsistency of feelings. Immorality. Unreliability. Mood swings. Dramatics. Lives in a world of fantasy. Out of touch with reality. Sex as bodily sensations. Victim mentality.

## Queen of Pentacles

Upper Levels: Feminine strength. Pragmatic. Practical and materialistic. Responsible. Fair and wise at business. Loves the good things in life and acquires them easily. Self-sufficient. Hardworking. Wealthy. Generous. Helpful friend or employer. Abundance. Luxury. Security. Liberty. Magnificence. Grace and dignity. Receptive. Sensuously enjoys pleasures of the body.

Lower Levels: False prosperity. Flaunts material possessions to gain approval from others. Suspicious. Neglects responsibilities. Vicious person. Untrusting. Fearful of failure. Jealousy. Sensual cravings. Compulsive. Hoarding.

# Knights

The images symbolize movement and action. They can stand for youth, though not as young as pages. They are seekers trying to reach a goal and are agents of change or catalysts.

## Knight of Swords

Upper Levels: Mercurial energy of the mind towards sudden inspiration or new ideas. Mental brilliance. Bravery. Heroic action. Rush into the unknown without fear.

Lower Levels: Pugnacity. Callousness. Takes no account of

others people's feelings. Ideas of hurting another. Needs constant mental stimuli. Mental agitation. Anger. Argumentative. War. Conceited. Disunion. Impulsivity. Imprudence. Cocky.

**Knight of Wands**

Upper Levels: Bravely going into the unknown or a journey. Attitude of purpose and confidence. Imagination. Intuitive. Sense of adventure. Generosity.

Lower Levels: Bad temper. Unfocused and cannot complete a task. Hyperactive. Changeable mind. Quarrelsome. Abrupt discontinuance of an activity. Bragging and self inflation.

**Knight of Cups**

Upper Levels: Like the Knights of the Holy Grail he has refined spiritual aspirations. Artistic high-principled youth. Idealistic seeker of love beauty and truth. His feeling life moves outward towards others. Courtly love of worshiping and idealizing women.

Lower Levels: Subtle trickery or deception. Fraud. A sly and cunning person. Playboy. Immature love. Emotional manipulator, playing on peoples emotions to gain an advantage.

**Knight of Pentacles**

Upper Levels: Hardworking materialist capable of succeeding at most goals. Mature and responsible. Reliable. Methodical. Persistent. Ability to finish a task. Laborious. Organized. Dependable. Patience and tolerance. Kind. Trustworthy. Nature loving.

Lower Levels: Black and white thinking. Stagnation. Carelessness. Spendthrift. Dogmatic views. Idleness. Lack of determination or direction. Lazy. Unimaginative. Has addictions.

## Pages

These images represent children, or an aspect of personality that is underdeveloped. They can symbolize the beginning of something new and undeveloped.

They may also represent servants, students, and apprentices still in the discovery mode.

### Page of Swords

Upper Levels: The beginnings of mental activity and formulation. Childlike curiosity. A person adept at perceiving. Discerning and uncovering the unknown. Insightful. Vigilant. Discreet. Alert to unknown dangers.

Lower Levels: An imposter. Powerlessness. Lack of preparation. Procrastination. Clever but unconcerned about the needs of others. Malicious. Cold and calculating. Spying for a deceitful purpose. Gossipy. Tendency to start petty quarrels.

### Page of Wands

Upper Levels: A faithful and loyal person. Consistent person. Bearer of important news. Trusted friend. Good intended stranger. Enthusiasm. Optimism. Student.

Lower Levels: Indecision. Reluctance. Instability. A gossip. Displeasure. Immature decision-making.

### Page of Cups

Upper Levels: The emergence of the capacity to feel. A renewed capacity to feel. Discovering that one is worthy of being loved. Sweetness. Gentleness. Birth of the creative imagination. Sensitive. Kind natured. Expressing strong artistic or psychic talents. Beginning to trust again.

Lower Levels: Vain self love. Infantile love. Obsessive love. Self-preoccupation. Egocentric. Passive dependency. Seduction. A flatterer. Emotional immaturity. Codependence.

**Page of Pentacles**

Upper Levels: Beginning awareness of the senses. Beginning capacity to manifest what they want in the world. Serious and studious. Careful. Hard-working. Diligent. Scholarship. Reflection. Deep concentration and application. Beginning to care for the body through better diet, exercise, relaxation.

Lower Levels: Unrealistic. Failure to face facts. Illogical thinking. Rebelliousness. Wastefulness. Fear of Loss. Fear of disapproval. Self-destructive. Attracted to pain.

---

**EXERCISE:** Working only with the court cards, do a series of readings for yourself. As you become familiar with the meanings I have given in this chapter, allow your intuition to create personal meanings as well.

**Sample questions to try:**
What qualities of my higher self do I tend to ignore?
What aspect of myself do I need to develop at this stage of my life?
What issues do I need to address in my relationship to [spouse, lover, friend, family, etc]?
What issues do I need to address at work?
What major archetype do I use at play?
What issues do I need to address to enrich my intimate relationships?

Chapter Eleven

# Levels of the Numbered Minor Arcana

*I Am Big*
*I Am Small*

The images on the numbered cards of the Minor Arcana represent archetypal behaviors and add detail to enhance the information of the layout. They symbolize scenarios we play out in our lives. Like the Major Arcana and the court cards, the archetypes of the situations depicted in the numbered cards can be acted out at an upper refined level or they can have a lower more primitive enactment. For example, Paul asked for a reading to help him with issues regarding a difficult relationship with his son. The card in the conscious position was the Four of Wands, which at the upper levels can represent tranquility in relationship. The card in the unconscious position was the Seven of Swords. At the upper level this numbered card can represent diplomacy. I knew we weren't working with the upper levels with Paul and his son.

The counseling session began by discussing the lower levels of the relationship between Paul and his son, which was mainly argumentative. The goal of the counseling process was to help Paul find his way to the more refined archetypal behaviors or solutions, which would bring about tranquility, compassion and peace.

I chose to focus upon the Seven of Swords, which appeared in the unconscious position of the layout. We explored Paul's negativity whenever he talked with his son, and I asked how he might bring more tranquility (upper level of the Four of Wands) into his relationship. Paul agreed to do more reality checking and active listening—diplomatic actions (upper level of the Seven of Swords) that would lead to a more balanced relationship.

Read through the card descriptions below noticing the numeric symbolic meanings assigned to each. I encourage you to do an exploration of the numbers on your own as you work with the cards. In this way you will have made sense of the numbers by using your own intuition and intellect. Trust the knowledge you gain through direct observation, objective analysis and active participation with the archetypal imagery and numbers of the cards.

## The Aces

The Aces indicate new beginnings of a positive and vigorous nature. They are symbolic of creative potential and indicate a tremendous surge of energy. It is the most intense archetypal energy of each suit. The other numbered cards derive their power from the Ace.

### Ace of Swords

Upper Levels: Mental authority that signifies progress and advancement of ideas. Great determination. Mental strength. Power. Championship. Conquest that follows a spiritual prime directive. Strength in adversity. Conflict brings new ideas and perspective.

Lower Levels: Tyrannical. Negative and self-destructive thinking. Violent temper. Embarrassment. Obstacles in planning. Hindrance. Mental infertility. Blocked thinking. Mental strife. Spiritual crisis due to intellectualization, which hinders the ability to feel.

### Ace of Wands

Upper Levels: Positive new beginnings with new ideas. Creativity. Initiative. New undertakings. Imagination. Ambition succeed. Strong sexual energy. Adventure. Invention. Enterprise. Beginning of a meaningful experience. Capacity to see future potential.

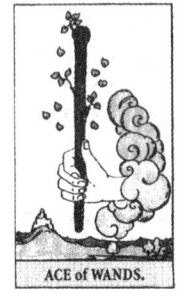

Lower Levels: Aborted beginning. Unrealized goal. Cancellation of plans. Impotence. Failure to trust imaginative possibilities. Undirected restlessness. Dissatisfaction with present circumstances. Hyperactivity.

### Ace of Cups

Upper Levels: The purest aspect of love's emotional energy. Divine energy behind the spiritual. The great journey of the heart. Noble love. Urge toward relationship and community. Pure spiritual feeling. Great abundance. Fulfillment. Perfection. Joy. Pleasure and happiness. Emotional growth. Loving union. Energy behind mystical experiences.

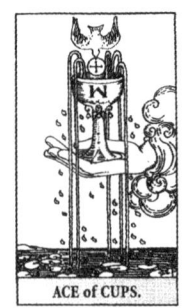

Lower Levels: Instability. Unrequited love. Insincere heart. Inconsistency. Loss of love. Unaware of intuitions of the heart and spiritual awareness.

### Ace of Pentacles

Upper Levels: The beginnings of material creation. Worldly wealth, status, and achievement. Success in business. Financial rewards. Prosperity. New and positive relationship. Ambition to create in the material world.

Lower Levels: Prosperity without happiness. Miserliness. Decadence. Greed. Misused wealth. Nothing happening on the material level. Poverty.

## The Twos

The Two symbolizes opposing forces and conflict. The number two reveals opposites: male and female, matter and spirit, positive and negative, etc.. The energy of the twos represents the potential co-creativity or a balance between opposing forces.

### Two of Swords

Upper Levels: A state of tension that is well balanced for the moment. A standstill with balanced forces immobilizing the situation. Harmony. Firmness. Receptivity. Courage. Peace. Meditation.

Lower Levels: Inharmonious balance. Conflict of opposing principles. Anxiety. Uncertainty. Procrastination. Passivity. Turning a blind eye to a situation. Falsehood. False friends. Lies. Treachery. Disloyalty.

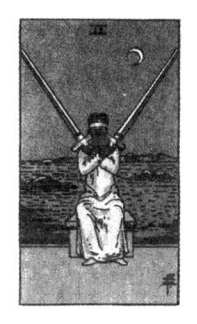

### Two of Wands

Upper Levels: A newly conceived goal or creative project. Looking towards future possibilities. Desiring new outlook from present environment. Desire for travel. High ideas and aims. Inspiration. Success through strength and vision. Courage in undertakings.

Lower Levels: Sadness. Loss of faith in self. Restrained by others. Unimaginative. Uninspired. No creative urges. Lack of a goal.

### Two of Cups

Upper Levels: Power of attraction. Well-balanced love or friendship. Beginning or renewed relationship. Understanding. Cooperation. Partnership. Marriage. A balance between spiritual and physical love. Resolution of quarrels. Harmony of opposites. Attraction of male and female. A sensual and spiritual seeking of the soul. Meetings and contractual arrangements between business partners.

Lower Levels: Separation. Divorce. False friendship. Troubled relationship. Misunderstanding. Opposition. Negative feelings due to loss of relationship.

**Two of Pentacles**

Upper Levels: Active and willing to try several things at once. The flexibility necessary to keep several propositions going at once. Flow of movement. Skillful manipulation that achieves success. Harmony within a change. Open to new ideas. Willingness to take risks to realize goals. A time of success in money matters. Going with the flow of events.

Lower Levels: Hoarding. Worry. Difficulty in launching new projects. Embarrassment. Anxiety about future. Lack of money. Trying to control the situation.

## The Threes

Threes symbolize creative growth and expansion. It is the number of initial completion a sign that the first step or stage has been achieved before the next can begin.

**Three of Swords**

Upper Levels: Sorrowful emotional storms with understanding and insight as a by-product. Sorrow put in perspective. Facing emotional upheaval with openness and honesty. Something that causes conflict to come to an end. A necessary painful state that helps to resolve self-delusion and blindness.

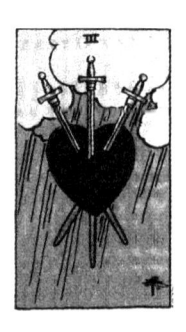

Lower Levels: Mental anxiety. Confusion. Unending sorrow. Feeling sorry for one's self. Lack of insight or understanding in a situation. Incompatibility. Separation. Disappointment. Strife and conflict. Heartbreak and loss.

**Three of Wands**

Upper Levels: After an initial completion of a goal, a decision has been made to proceed further. A satisfaction of achievement. A challenge of things to come. New creative ideas. Optimism and a feeling of satisfaction about a project. A time of waiting for the next opportunity or news. Enterprise. Negotiations. Trade. Commerce.

Lower Levels: Assistance with an ulterior motive. Treachery. Impatience. Poor timing in a project. Poor planning. Uncertainty. Insecurity. Lack of new ideas.

**Three of Cups**

Upper Levels: A celebration of emotional fulfillment. Completion of an initial attraction. Celebration of a marriage. A situation of emotional fulfillment and promise. Healing.

Lower Levels: Excessive pleasures. Overabundance. Unappreciative. Loss of prestige. Broken promises. Failed relationship. One-sided illusionary relationship.

**Three of Pentacles**

Upper Levels: Completing the first stages of a project. Commitment towards completion. Work required in relationships. Mastery of a skill. Artistic ability. Material gains that work brings.

Lower Levels: Sloppiness. Mediocrity. Lower quality. Money problems. Lack of skill. Commonplace ideas. Lack of commitment.

## The Fours

Four symbolizes completion and equality. It is the number of reality, logic, and reason, bringing together a state of cooperation and stability on the material plane.

**Four of Swords**

Upper Levels: A time of rest and reflection after a struggle. A quiet period for thinking things through. Release of tension and anxiety. Time of relaxation or recuperation. Withdrawal and contemplation. Prayer and meditation. Peaceful negotiations.

Lower Levels: Abandonment. Precaution. Guarded advancement. Loneliness. Time of anxiety and stillness. Unruly negotiations.

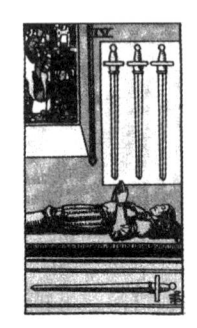

**Four of Wands**

Upper Levels: Completion. Happy, productive energy and growth. Celebration after labor. Harvest and reward. Restful pause in activities. Vacation. Holidays. Romance. Peace and tranquility. Cooperative group. Community.

Lower Levels: Loss of tranquility. Insecurity. Incomplete happiness. Unfulfilled romance. Anxiety over loss. Negative politics. Disruption of community.

**Four of Cups**

Upper Levels: Looking at life in a fresh way. Positive possibilities. New relationships. Acquiring emotional knowledge. New approaches to old problems.

Lower Levels: Discontentment. Boredom. Confusion. Unable to see opportunities offered.

Emotional funk. Disappointment. Bitter experience. Stagnation.

**Four of Pentacles**

Upper Levels: Strength of purpose in monetary matters. Good investments. Clear boundaries. Right relationship. Strong foundation in relationships. Personal power. Ability to take care of one's domain. Ability to apply one's full power in a practical and tangible way.

Lower Levels: Miserliness. Greed. Hoarder. Inability to share. Insecurity. Selfishness. Setbacks in material holdings. Suspense and delay. Poor boundaries. Difficult relationship.

## The Fives

Five is active and unstable, and may change or shift without notice. It is inconsistant and causes uncertainty, evolving into either creativity or chaos.

**Five of Swords**

Upper Levels: Swallowing self-pride. Accepting limitations before taking action in a new direction. Acceptance of what you cannot change. Acceptance of mistakes and learning from them. Creative endeavors.

Lower Levels: Denial. Defeat. Fear of being hurt again. Negative thinking patterns. Dishonor. Destruction of others through rumors. Self-destructive behaviors.

**Five of Wands**

Upper Levels: Surmounting petty obstacles. Overcoming difficulty in communication. Energy being held back appropriately. Desiring full expression. Accommodating limitations of practical life. Obstacles that arise in the course of creative work. Gut sense of timing, feeling how the laws of the material world operate. Compromises.

Lower Levels: Feeling limited, restricted or restrained. Nothing working in play or work. Anxiety. Frustration. Strife. Unsatisfied desires. Obstacles. Conflict. Contradictions. Minor health issues.

**Five of Cups**

Upper Levels: Exploring alternatives within loss. Counting your blessings during a time of grief. Hopeful outlook. Favorable expectations. New alliances. Reunion. Acceptance of imperfection. Self-transformation through difficulties and disappointments. Salvaging a partially lost relationship.

Lower Levels: Emotional negativity. Partial loss. Friendship without heart. Marriage without heart. Disappointment. Fragile. Vulnerable. Regret over past actions. Betrayal. Self-betrayal.

**Five of Pentacles**

Upper Levels: Seeking spiritual direction in a time of despair. The dark before the dawn. Unsanctioned love and affection. Discovering personal power. Releasing worry about material concerns. Creativity in community projects.

Lower Levels: Worry over material concerns. Over-identification with material success. Anxiety over money matters. Financial hard times. Lost spiritual or religious direction. Loss of faith in oneself. Survival issues. Sexual promiscuity.

## The Sixes

Six represents balance, harmony, and equilibrium. It is two sets of threes working side-by-side symbolizing a time of focused balance of the suit.

### Six of Swords

Upper Levels: Moving away from difficulties to a more peaceful time. A sense of harmony after a period of tension and anxiety. Moving to a more peaceful environment. A peaceful and tranquil mind. Acceptance of limitations. Observing with a fair, witnessing mind. Insight and understanding.

Lower Levels: Stalemate. Confession. Inability to learn from mistakes. Lack of insight and understanding. Blaming others.

### Six of Wands

Upper Levels: Achievement of one's hopes and wishes. Success and the satisfaction it brings. Rewards for effort expended towards a good cause. Conquest. Triumph. Good news. Public validation of creative vision or work.

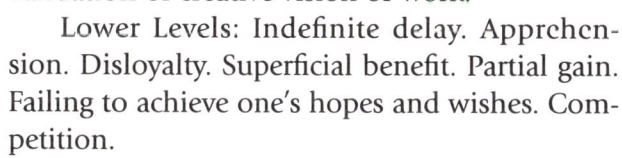

Lower Levels: Indefinite delay. Apprehension. Disloyalty. Superficial benefit. Partial gain. Failing to achieve one's hopes and wishes. Competition.

### Six of Cups

Upper Levels: Feeling good about home and childhood memories. Pleasure derived from being with an old friend. Emotional pleasure that is healing and deeply nurturing. Inner contentment.

Lower Levels: Lives in the past. Sentimental fantasy that is untrue. Self-recrimination about past deeds. Difficulty accepting limitations of reality.

### Six of Pentacles
Upper Levels: Success. Sharing. Loving generosity. Financial affairs are stable. Gracious acceptance of the generosity of others. Physical attainment. Accomplishment. Productivity. Following what has heart and meaning in life.

Lower Levels: Unsuccessful. Conditional generosity. Poverty. Self-absorption. Jealousy. Ungiving of one's self. Unpaid loans. Envy.

## The Sevens
The seven is symbolic of wisdom relating to the completion of cycles or completion of a phase. It is a time to take stock of what has happened and move forward.

### Seven of Swords
Upper Levels: Moral integrity in diplomacy. Prudence. Mental prowess. Wit. Tactfully stated ideas in politics. New plans. Fantasy. Cautious efforts.

Lower Levels: Evasion in order to gain an objective. Flight from a dishonorable act. Guilt. Guile and cunning. Cold and manipulative. Deliberate charm to gain from others. Arguments. Uncertain counsel or advice. Slander. Babble. Lies.

### Seven of Wands
Upper Levels: An evenly matched struggle. Creative group vision and hard work toward a goal. Ambition and competitive instincts for the collective good. Success. Overcoming obstacles

and challenges. Advantage. Victory. Travel or moves.

Lower Levels: Envy. Competition. Ambitions to further ego needs. Anxiety. Embarrassment. Indecision. Hesitancy causing losses. Uncertainty.

**Seven of Cups**

Upper Levels: Choices of the heart. Happy fantasies. Rosy vision of the future. An emotional situation in which many possibilities are evident. Desire and will. Abundance of creative artistic talent. Decisive.

Lower Levels: Illusions. Unrealistic attitudes. Wishful unrealistic fantasies. Obsessive desire. Wanting ego gratification. Indecision.

**Seven of Pentacles**

Upper Levels: A pause during the development of an enterprise. Assessment. Thoughtful decision-making. Sensible choices. Divine vision. Choices that oppose popular beliefs. New possibility containing potential for growth. Money. Wealth. Gain.

Lower Levels: Compulsive decisions. Stagnation resulting from making safe choices instead of following intuition and vision. Immorality. Impatience. Imprudent actions. Loss of money. Unwise investments.

## The Eights

The Eight symbolizes regeneration and balance of opposing forces. It bespeaks of the death of the old and outdated making way for the new and relevant.

**Eight of Swords**

Upper Levels: Gestation of new ideas. New paradigm. Analytical thinking. Honestly facing the truth in a situation. Caution due to full knowledge and consequences of a situation. Acceptance of consequences.

Lower Levels: A situation that is binding and restricting. Fear and indecision. Painful consciousness of one's own part in creating the difficult situation. Dilemma. Impasse. Depressed state of mind. Illness. Imprisonment. Criticism. Accident.

**Eight of Wands**

Upper Levels: Sudden burst of creative energy. Increase in creative imagination. New activities and new beginnings. Time for initiative and action to begin. Busy and exciting time ahead. Travel and moves. Sudden progress. Triumph over obstacles. Direct communication.

Lower Levels: Quarrels. Discord. Stagnation. Jealousy. Harassment. Dispute. Hastily made decisions. Blocked imagination and creativity. Procrastination. Covert communication.

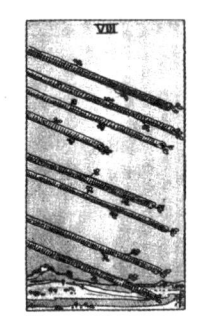

**Eight of Cups**

Upper Levels: Accepting what one cannot change and moving on. Modesty. Happiness. Emotional effort continued until success is attained. Festivity. Joy. Feasting. Giving up and starting anew. Transformation of old attitudes. Moving into the unknown with faith.

Lower Levels: Disappointment. Disillusion. Dissatisfaction. Discontinuance of effort. Abandonment of plans. Grief. Depressed mood. Tired. Emotionally drained.

**Eight of Pentacles**

Upper Levels: Craftsmanship. Enthusiastic about work. Turning a skill or talent into money or a profession. New employment. Hard work and practical ideas. Apprenticeship. Enthusiasm for a new trade. Dedication. Spirit of adventure. Turning a hobby into a paying proposition. Moving through fears of failure and fears of success.

Lower Levels: Lack of ambition. Vanity. Conceit. Disillusionment. Hypocrisy. Fear of failure. Fear of success. Feeling of limitation.

## The Nines

Nine contains the archetypal principle of strength and determination, which a persona needs to complete a task or goal.

### Nine of Swords

Upper Levels: Intense inner work. Acceptance of the shadow aspect of yourself or another. Objective self-criticism. Letting go of guilt from the past. Accepting fears. Acknowledgement of negative thinking patterns. Reasonable fears. Vitality in thinking. Intense communication. Brainstorming.

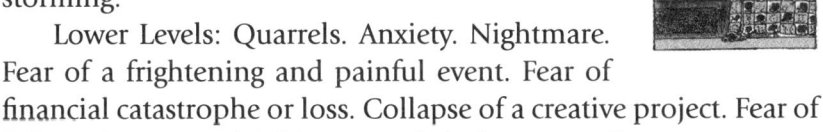

Lower Levels: Quarrels. Anxiety. Nightmare. Fear of a frightening and painful event. Fear of financial catastrophe or loss. Collapse of a creative project. Fear of failure. Negative thinking. Harsh judgments of self and others. Worry. Suffering. Despair. Doubt. Suspicion or paranoia. Slanderous gossip. Shame. Timidity. Shady character.

### Nine of Wands

Upper Levels: Spiritual and intuitive strength of vision. Mental, emotional, spiritual and physical strength. Ability to handle difficult situations.

Strength of will over animal nature. Willpower. Reserve strength. The injection of new hope. New ideas into a situation. Gaining new energy after a period of exhaustion.

Lower Levels: Obstacles. Adversity. Problems. Delays. Displeasure. Barriers to overcome. Ill health. Expectation of difficulties and changes. Awaiting tribulation. A pause in a current struggle.

**Nine of Cups**

Upper Levels: Happiness that is associated with health, finances, work creativity or relationships. Internal and external fulfillment. Happiness experienced in the mind, body and spirit. Contentment. Well-being. Abundance. Difficulties surmounted. Good health. Forgiveness.

Lower Levels: Mistakes. Material and emotional loss. Spiritual crisis. Dispute. Misplaced truth. Resentment. Despair. Depression.

**Nine of Pentacles**

Upper Levels: Material well-being. Pleasure in physical comfort and material success. Finding pleasure in being alone with the self. Solitary contemplative time. Self-satisfaction. Prosperity. Security. Family matters. Home. Love of nature. Gain after following what has heart and meaning.

Lower Levels: Possible loss. Loss of material possessions. Robbery. Gambling. Poor judgment in money matters. Poverty.

## The Tens

The number ten represents the archetypal principle of perfection through completion. The cycle is completed and is ready to begin again with the Ace.

## Ten of Swords

Upper Levels: The decision to end one thing to make way for something new. Acceptance of the change. The final straw. An ending that is accomplished through fairness and good judgment. Truth becomes clear. Proper and inevitable completion of a process. Release of suffering. Beneficial gain.

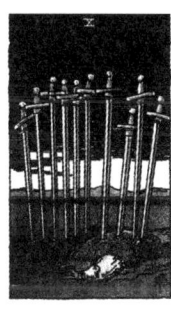

Lower Levels: Fear of ruin. Fear of the end of a relationship. Anxiety about finances. Abrupt change heralding unknown circumstances. Despair. Exhaustion. Disillusionment and disappointment. Grief. Sorrow. Mental anguish

## Ten of Wands

Upper Levels: Accepting limitation. Accepting responsibilities. Creating unconventional and creative outlets for an otherwise oppressive situation. Creatively resisting outdated cultural dogma in the home and workplace. Problems create a time for change and new ideas.

Lower Levels: Oppression. Holding back self-expression. Burdened. Weight of worldly responsibilities. Overburdened. Excessive pressures. Using power for selfish ends. Competition. Jealousy. Confinement.

## Ten of Cups

Upper Levels: Emotional contentment and satisfaction. Love that encompasses the personal, sensual and spiritual. Ecstasy. An open heart. Life with meaning and purpose. Permanence in the realm of the heart. Home. Happiness. Joy. Love. Pleasure. Virtue. Honor. Self-esteem. Impeccable reputation.

Lower Levels: Loss of friendship. Unhappiness. Family disputes. Rage. Pettiness. Strife. Opposition. Unrequited love. Emotional conflict.

**Ten of Pentacles**

Upper Levels: Abundance. Prosperity. Wealth. Ability to manifest abundance. Security. Good friends. Family matters. Peak conversation. Inheritance. Home. Situation of permanence. Satisfaction that one has built something for future generations. Buying and selling of property. Living life fully.

Lower Levels: Poor risk. Bad odds. Loss. Bankruptcy. Gambling. Hazardous conditions. Illness. Loss of inheritance. Controlling.

---

**EXERCISE:**

Using only the numbered cards, shuffle and ask a question about a situation. Spread the first four cards out in a line on the table and practice reading them. Give a friend or a family member a practice reading

# Epilogue

*I Am All That is…*
*I Am the All.*

A feeling of quiet satisfaction comes to me as I bring this book to an end. Once more, I turn to my Voyager deck of cards to seek a final blessing – for myself, and for you, my readers. I draw the "Child of Wands" — also entitled "Seeker" — and it is filled with images of peace: Buddhist monks, a deer, a man in a forest, a gentle wolf, a mouse, and a smiling child hunter with spears resting in his hand. In the center of the card there is a small cross-legged figure, meditating. The deck's author, James Wanless, states:

> Life is a path of seeking self-discovery. To seek your truth is to see. Try to see it all. Look at everything because you are everything. Find the eternal truths by looking at the world about you, and find yourself in the process. Use your physical senses to sense the truth. Use the great teachings to ponder and learn the truth. Use your meditative introspection to know the truth.
>
> Like the child hunter, be diligent and preserving in your pursuit of truth. Never stop looking. You must be a warrior—full of courage to hunt down the truth amidst the dark shadow-demons. Trust your self and your inner sense, for the path to truth can only be your individual path. Trust the strength of the "path to enlightenment" to

overcome all dark forces.

We are all warriors, searching for inner wisdom and peace, and for those who embrace the spiritual path, Tarot brings many rewards, helping us gain access to our intuition and the archetypal richness that fills our inner and outer worlds as we partake of the hero's journey, the journey we all must take as we strive for consciousness and joy.

# Appendix A

# The Reversed Tarot Card

Occasionally a reversed card (where the image is upside-down) will show up in a Tarot spread. Many books on Tarot give relevance to reversed cards, and the meaning that is attributed to such cards is often the opposite of the meaning given when the card appears right-side-up. In my own practice, however, I do not give much credence to reversed cards. When it has meaning, I see it as indicating the lower levels of the archetype or a situation that has not yet happened. If I feel that it indicates the lower levels of an archetype, I begin the therapeutic discussion by listing the attributes I described in chapters Nine, Ten and Eleven then focusing on the process of elevating the client's the consciousness towards the upper levels of that same archetype. For example, Ellen, a nurse, was seeking professional advice. She chose the Voyager deck to ask the question "Who am I, professionally?" One of the cards in her layout was the reversed "Fortune," number X of the Major Arcana. Traditionally, the Wheel of Fortune represents the archetypal principle of opportunity, abundance and prosperity. Ellen identified with the image of a black woman sitting cross-legged with a crystal in her lap as a healer. A golden hand reaching towards the woman represented her desire to be more professionally fulfilled.

Ellen was employed in a job that wouldn't allow her to use her talents as a holistic nurse. Since she desired a job with heart and meaning, I saw the reversed card as representing a lack of opportunity.

The next card, the "Moon," number XVIII was also reversed. Traditionally the Moon represents an inner consciousness seeking authentic expression. Ellen identified with the image of a wolf howling at the moon. "This is me," she said, "Trying to communicate what I know to others."

The reversed card reminded me of the lower levels of the archetype: a situation that wasn't happening. Ellen wasn't able to communicate authentically and was not in a position to satisfactorily express herself at work. We explored how she could improve her situation in order to gain authentic expression found at the upper levels of the archetype.

# Appendix B

# Tarot Research

Culberson, M.J.C. (1982). *The Relationship Between Transpersonal Symbols: Dreams and Tarot*. Unpublished doctoral dissertation, Institute of Transpersonal Psychology, California.

Dr. Culberson presented a dissertation investigating the relationship between inner dream symbols, received through dream incubation, and external waking symbols illustrated through the media of Tarot. The hypothesis she set forth and experimentally tested was that the symbols of dreams and Tarot are archetypally connected. They come from the same unconscious realm, and therefore, the symbols of both an incubated dream and a focused Tarot spread for a given individual at a given point in time will reflect the same themes, issues and content.

In the study there were twelve subjects, each of whom completed two dream/Tarot packets. They had been recording their dreams for at least one year prior to this study. All but one subject were familiar with the techniques of dream incubation, and had previously experimented with asking for guidance from their dreams. Most reported success at receiving guidance.

Rating was done on both the dreams and the Tarot spreads on a seven-point scale in relationship to their incubation questions. All dream packet data were presented along with the correct Tarot spread and three false spreads to a panel of three judges who were all adept at reading Tarot.

The judges blindly ranked and rated the four Tarot spreads on how well they matched the dream using a seven-point scale. This information was statistically analyzed.

This data was evidence that something other than random chance was operating in the judges' ability to correctly match the Tarot spread chosen by the subject with the dream and incubation issue for the subject.

The Jungian concept of synchronicity was set forth as a theoretical explanation for the statistically significant judging results. Dr.. Culberson stated that the judges were able to perceive similar or identical symbols and the similar symbolic messages in the dream and Tarot spread for the twenty-four dream/Tarot sets they studied (see Tables 1, 2, and 3).

The conclusion supported the hypothesis that the symbols of dreams and Tarot are archetypally connected. They come from the same unconscious realm and the psyche can speak through either form.

Dr. Culberson also reported the subjects' rating of their own dreams and Tarot spreads in relationship to their incubation questions, concluding that the incubated dreams and focused Tarot spreads were found to be related to the incubation questions.

Thus the dream/Tarot process was found to be a positive, useful, therapeutic tool. She also suggested that it was a potent way to evaluate an individual's current psychological issues.

Finally, Dr. Culbertson concluded that the visual experiencing of dreams and Tarot images could be a dynamic aid to meditation narrowing down the psychic field of vision and focusing it on a particular symbol for the purpose of self-immersion and realization of one's inner experience.

At the same time, these symbols serve to produce an inner order providing safe refuge for healing and self-actualization.

### Figure 3, Table 1

#### Tarot Spread Rankings

| Judge | No. 1 ranking for correct Tarot spread | Ranking below No. 1 for correct spread | Total | Direct Hits* | Hits** | Misses*** |
|---|---|---|---|---|---|---|
| No. 1 | 10 | 14 | 24 | 4 | 14 | 10 |
| No. 2 | 13 | 11 | 24 | 6 | 15 | 9 |
| No. 3 | 11 | 13 | 24 | 6 | 14 | 10 |
| Total | 34 | 38 | 72 | 16 | 43 | 29 |

Total units of data from all three judges = 72

\* A Direct Hit is defined as placement of the correct Tarot spread in the top category (i.e., A: Very Great Correspondence).
\*\* A Hit is defined as placement of the correct Tarot spread within the top two categories (i.e., A: Very Great Correspondence and B: Great Correspondence).

\*\*\* A Miss is defined as placement of the correct Tarot spread in the last five categories (i.e., C: Moderate Correspondence through G: No Correspondence).

### Figure 3, Table 2

## Ranking Statistical Results

| Judge | No. 1 ranking for correct Tarot spread |  | Ranking below No. 1 for correct spread |  | _2 | P(one tailed) |
|---|---|---|---|---|---|---|
|  | Observed | Expected | Observed | Expected |  |  |
| No. 1 | 10 | 6 | 14 | 18 | 2.72 | <.05 |
| No. 2 | 13 | 6 | 11 | 18 | 9.39 | <.01 |
| No. 3 | 11 | 6 | 13 | 18 | 4.5 | <.02 |

### Figure 3, Table 2

## Tarot Spread Ratings

|  | Mean Rating Correct | Mean Rating Incorrect | D | t | df | p |
|---|---|---|---|---|---|---|
| Trial 1 | 2.79 | 4.38 | +1.59 | +3.28 | 11 | <.01 |
| Trial 2 | 2.89 | 3.95 | +1.07 | +1.99 | 11 | <.05 |
| Trail 3 | 2.84 | 4.16 | +1.32 | +3.26 | 11 | <.01 |

# Recommended Resources

I use the following decks, which are readily available through most bookstores or the internet. Most of the decks listed come with a book or pamphlet with information about the author's perspective. The decks I have chosen for clients have symbols that are easy to relate to, whereas the decks I recommend for personal use are more complex, offering greater enrichment for the skilled reader.

*With Clients:*
The Osho Zen
The Voyager
The Mythic Tarot with book by Sharman-Burke & Greene
Morgan-Greer Tarot
Aquarian Tarot
Sacred Rose Tarot
The Medieval Scapini Tarot
The New Paladini
Golden Tarot of the Tsar
*Personal Inner Work:*
All of the above decks plus:
Tarot of Spirit
The Haindl Tarot
Waite-Rider

# Recommended CD ROM

I highly recommend the following discs, which are available through the web site www.tarot.com. They are particularly useful for self readings.

Tarot Magic. Visionary Networks, Portland Oregon
By Tarot Scholar Christine Payne-Towler
The Oracle of Changes: Visionary Networks, Portland Oregon

MESSAGES FROM THE ARCHETYPES

# Interactive Guided Imagery<sup>sm</sup> Training

**Nurses Certificate Program in Imagery**
**Beyond Ordinary Nursing**
**PO Box 8177**
**Foster City, CA 94404-3004**
**Web site: www.imageryrn.com**
**(605) 570-6157**

**Academy of Guided Imagery**
**PO Box 2070**
**Mill Valley, CA 94942**
**www.healthy.net**
**(415) 389-9325**

# Selected Bibliography

Arrien, A. (1987). *The Tarot Handbook: Practical Application of Ancient Visual Symbols.* Sonoma, CA: Arcus Publishing company.

Bolen, J. S. (1979). *The Tao of Psychology: Synchronicity and the Self.* San Francisco: Harper and Row Publishers.

Burger, E., Fiebig, J. (1997) *Complete Book of Tarot Spreads.* New York, NY: Sterling Publishing Co.

Cowan, D. (1996). *A Gift for Healing: How You Can Use Therapeutic Touch.* New York: Crown Paperback Books.

Douglas, Alfred. (1972). *The Tarot: The Origins, Meaning and Uses of the Cards.* New York: Penguin Books.

Ferrucci, P. (1982). *What We May Be: Techniques for Psychological and Spiritual Growth through Psychosynthesis.* New York: G.P. Putnam's Sons.

Gallo, F. P. (1999). *Energy Psychology: Explorations at the Interface of Energy, Cognition, Behavior, and Health.* New York: N. Y., CRC Press.

Godwin, J. (1979). *Athanasius Kircher: A Renaissance Man and the Quest for Lost Knowledge.* London, Great Britton: Thames and Hudson.

Godwin, J. (1991). *Robert Fludd: hermetic philosopher and surveyor of two worlds.*

Grand Rapids, MI: Phanes Press.

Goleman, D. (1988). *The Meditative Mind: The Varieties of Meditative Experience.* New York: J.P. Putnam Sons.

Goswami, A. (1995). *Self Aware Universe: How Consciousness Creates the Material World.* New York: J. Tarcher/ Putnam.

Grof, S., Bennett, H. (1993) *The Holotropic Mind: The Three Levels of Human Consciousness and How They Shape our Lives.* San Francisco, CA: Harper Collins Publishers.

Gwain, R. (1994). *Discovering Yourself Through Tarot: A Jungian Guide to Archetypes and Personality.* Rochester VT: Destiny Books.

Hall, M. P. (1962) *The Secret Teachings of All Ages: An Encyclopedic Outline of Masonic, Hermetic, Cabbalistic and Rosicrucian Symbolical Philosophy.* Los Angeles, CA: The Philosophical Research Society, Inc.

Jette,C. (2001). *Tarot for the Healing Heart: Using Inner Wisdom to Heal Body and Mind.* St. Paul, MI, Llewellyn Publications.

Jung, C.G. (1969). Synchronicity: An Acausal Connecting Principle. *Collected Works of C. G. Jung, 8,* Bollingen Series 20. Princeton, NJ: Princeton University Press.

Kaplan, S.R. (1978). *The Encyclopedia of Tarot,* New York: U.S. Games Systems, Inc. Publishers.

Kaplan, S.R. (1972). *Tarot Classic.* Stamford, CT: U.S. Games Systems, Inc. Publishers.

Lawlis, F. et al (1996). *Transpersonal Medicine: A New Approach to Healing Body-Mind-Spirit.* Boston, MA: Shambhala.

Maslow, A. (1968). *Toward A Psychology of Being.* New York: Van Nostrand Reinold.

Payne-Towler, C. (1999). *The Underground Stream: Esoteric Tarot Revealed.* Eugene, Oregon: Noreah Press.

Pearson, C. (1991). *Awakening the Heroes Within: Twelve Archetypes to Help Us Find Ourselves and Transform Our World.* New York, N.Y.: Harper San Francisco.

Peat, D.F. (1987). *Synchronicity—The Bridge Between Matter and Mind.* New York: Bantam Books.

Rosengarten, A (2000). *Tarot and Psychology: Spectrums of Possibility.* St. Paul, MI: Paragon House.

Rossman, M., Bresler, D. (1992) *Interactive guided Imagery: Clinical Techniques for Brief Therapy and Health Psychology.* 6th Ed. Mill valley, CA, Academy for Guided Imagery, Inc. Publisher.

Sharman-Burke, J. (1996). *The Complete Book of Tarot.* New York: St. Martin's Griffin.

Sharman-Burke, J., Greene, L. (2000). *The Mythic Tarot: A New Approach to the Tarot Cards.* New York, NY: A Fireside Book, by Simon & Schuster.

Vaughn, F. E. (1979). *Awakening Intuition*. New York, NY: Doubleday, Anchor Books.

Wilber, K. (2000). *Integral Psychology: Consciousness, Spirit, Psychology, Therapy*. Boston: Shambhala.

Wirth, O. (1990). *The Tarot of the Magicians*. York Beach, MN, Samuel Weiser, Inc.

REPRINTED TAROT IMAGES
Tarot Images reprinted with permission from:
Osho International, images/text taken from the *Osho Zen Tarot: The Transcendental Game of Zen*, by Osho. 1995 St. Martin's Press, New York ISBN 0312117337
Online reading available at www.osho.com

*Voyager Tarot: Way of the Great Oracle*, by James Wanless and artist Ken Knutson. Merrill-West Publishing, Carmel, CA. Available online at www.voyagertarot.com

Illustrations from the Rider-Waite Tarot Deck, known also as the Rider Tarot and the Waite Tarot, reproduced by permission of U.S. Games Systems, Inc., Stamford, CT 06902 USA. Copyright 1971 by U.S. Games Systems, Inc. Further reproduction prohibited. The Rider-Waite Tarot Deck is a registered trademark of U.S. Games Systems, Inc. www.usgamesinc.com

THE AUTHOR
Toni Gilbert, RN, MA, HNC is a certified holistic nurse with a practice in transpersonal counseling. She has a bachelor's degree in psychology and art and continued her interest in art and its symbolism in a graduate school. She holds a master's degree in transpersonal studies from the Institute of Transpersonal Psychology. As a professional with certifications in Wellness Counseling, Mind-Body Consciousness, The Uses of Imagery in Medicine and Interactive Guided Imagery$^{sm}$, she offers clients an array of healing arts techniques. She owns Centre of Main St., a wellness center in Jefferson, Oregon. She can be reached through her web site at www.tonigilbert.com

THE EDITOR
Mark Robert Waldman is a therapist and author of nine books and anthologies, including *The Art of Staying Together, The Spirit of Writing, Dreamscaping* and the four-volume series, *Archetypes of the Collective Unconscious: Shadow, Healer, Seeker, Lover.* He was the founding editor of the *Transpersonal Review* and is chairman of the Los Angeles Transpersonal Interest Group.